Brookes Cooks

Susan Brookes

Boxtree

First published in the UK 1990 by Boxtree Limited
36 Tavistock Street
London WC2E 7PB

1 3 5 7 9 10 8 6 4 2

Published in association with
Granada Television/This Morning

Designed by ML Design
Photography by Bryan Winstanley/The Manchester
Picture Company
Home Economist Sue Norman
Line drawings by Laura Cream

Printed and bound by Billing & Sons Limited, Worcester

British Library Cataloguing in Publication Data
Brookes, Susan
Brookes cooks this morning
1. Food-Recipes
I. Title II. Series
641.5
ISBN 1-85283-085-9

CONTENTS

INTRODUCTION

BROOKES COOKS

THIS MORNING

BY SUSAN BROOKES

You might wonder how it comes about that I am cooking on television when it's quite widely known that I was thrown out of cookery classes at school - for talking.

It is because it used to annoy me that the only sort of food you saw on TV was very expensive and extravagant, done to impress rather than give some practical ideas for people who have a family or friends to feed in a hurry.

So I suggested a more down-to-earth approach which became *On the Market* - some of you may remember this being shown on Wednesday afternoons. They were four very happy busy years, and when the chance came to do something similar on *This morning*, I thought I might well enjoy that, too. And I was right. Well, after we'd got things sorted out a bit - we started by assembling a salad on the studio floor the first morning as no one had thought that we might need somewhere to chop up the lettuce while another item was being done in the nice new kitchen set.

The recipes in the book are some of the ones that have proved popular when we did them on the programme, and there are lots of new ideas for you to try. Use either all metric or all imperial measurements. Eggs are size 3, spoonfuls are level unless otherwise stated. Do remember that oven temperatures vary a lot, and if yours is a bit fast or slow, you may need to adjust the cooking times.

I've tried to indicate how many people I think a recipe will serve, but my family have hearty appetites so they may by only a rough guide. At our house, everyone cooks, and my biggest problem on some days is trying to elbow husband and daughters out so I can get to the stove.

In case you think you can tell what the Brookes are having for supper be seeing what's cooking on *This Morning*, I'll let you into a secret - the food never gets as far as home. The moment the cameras move away, the gannets are in there grazing; the crew is very hungry by 12 o'clock! Sometimes it can happen too early, as once when I had planned to poach four pears in red wine and found there were only three in the fruit bowl – Richard had walked past and swiped one when I wasn't looking and had eaten most of it before I could stop him.

I hope everyone can find something to enjoy both cooking and eating in this book. Food is fun - what else gives you the chance to be creative, give everyone a treat and enjoy it yourself as well? Happy cooking!

Susan Brookes

SOUPS & STARTERS

MELON WITH STILTON AND WATERCRESS SAUCE

Ingredients

4 oz (110 g) Stilton cheese
I bunch watercress
I small carton natural yoghurt
a little lemon juice

Don't be boring and serve a wedge of melon with a cherry stuck on top - try this, as the flavours really work well together, and it is simple so you can't go wrong. A whole honeydew melon will serve 4-6 people, and with this sauce it is posh enough for a dinner party.

Instructions

Preparation

Put the watercress, rinsed under cold water, into a food processor bowl or liquidiser with the Stilton from which you have removed the rind. Process for a few seconds until all the ingredients are well mixed together.

Add the yoghurt and a squeeze of lemon juice, and mix together. Chill this sauce in the fridge - it will thicken nicely if left to stand - and prepare the melon.

Presentation

I serve the peeled and de-seeded melon wedges in 2 or 3 crescent-shaped slices on a plate with 2 or 3 spoonfuls of the sauce in the curve of the slices. A leaf of watercress as garnish helps it to look good - very nouvelle cuisine!

SPICED APPLE SOUP

SOUPS & STARTERS

TIME NEEDED 1 hr

SERVES 6 PEOPLE

Ingredients

1½ lb (700 g) crisp dessert apples
1 medium onion, chopped
1 stick celery
2 oz (50 g) butter
1 teaspoon (5 ml) medium curry powder
¼ pint (150 ml) dry sherry
1 pint (600 ml) vegetable stock

Instructions

Preparation

Wash and core the apples, peel and chop the onion, and trim the celery.

Cooking

Melt the butter in a pan and sauté the roughly chopped apple with the onion, celery and curry powder for 3 minutes. Add the sherry, cover the pan, and leave to simmer for 20 minutes.

Take off the heat, and put into a liquidiser or food processor, and purée until smooth. Add the stock, heat gently, and check the seasoning - you may not need to add any.

Presentation

This soup looks nice served with a dash of Greek yoghurt or cream and a few apple slices in each bowl.

SUSAN'S HOT BORTSCH

SOUPS & STARTERS

TIME NEEDED 1¼ hrs

SERVES 6 PEOPLE

Ingredients

3 medium sized beetroot (raw)
1 large carrot, diced
1 onion, finely chopped
4 oz (110 g) white cabbage, shredded
2 pints (1¼ litres) beef stock
2 tablespoons lemon juice or vinegar
1 oz (25 g) butter
salt and pepper
sour cream for garnishing
6 tablespoons dry sherry (optional)
chives (optional)

Instructions

Preparation

Finely chop or process the beetroot, onion, cabbage and carrot. Sauté the chopped vegetables in the melted butter in a large saucepan. Add the stock, lemon juice or vinegar.

Cooking

Simmer the soup for about 30 minutes until the vegetables are tender. For a smooth consistency, process or liquidise the soup. Add the sherry, if required, and season to taste.

Presentation

Bortsch is eaten with a dash of sour cream and garnished with chopped chives. It can be served hot or chilled.

MUSHROOM PÂTÉ

Ingredients

8 oz *(225 g) mushrooms*

1 small onion

4 oz (110 g) butter

1 oz (25 g) wholewheat breadcrumbs

4 oz (110 g) cream cheese or cottage cheese (sieved)

a pinch of nutmeg

1 clove garlic

Instructions

Preparation

Finely chop the onion and mushrooms.

Cooking

Fry together in the butter until soft. Stir in the breadcrumbs and all remaining ingredients. Pour into a buttered pâté dish and chill.

Presentation

Serve with melba toast.

TOMATO AND BASIL SOUP

Ingredients

½ an onion, chopped

1 lb (450 g) tomatoes

1 oz (25 g) butter

2 or 3 sprigs fresh basil or ½ teaspoon dried

¾ pint (425 ml) chicken stock

¼ pint single cream or top of milk

salt and pepper amd sugar to taste

This soup freezes well, so it is worth making in large quantities towards the end of summer, when tomatoes are cheap.

Instructions

Preparation

Melt the butter in a pan, peel and chop the onion, and fry gently in the butter for a couple of minutes until it softens. Roughly chop the tomatoes - quartering them will do.

Cooking

Add to the pan, stir, cover the pan, and let them stew for a couple of minutes. If you are using a stock cube (as they are so salty, I would only use half of one), crumble it into the pan and then add ¾ pint (425 ml) of the water. When you have added the stock, simmer for 5 minutes, then add the dried or chopped basil, and simmer for another 5 minutes. Take off the heat, and liquidise the soup until smooth. Put it back in the pan and reheat, taste and then add seasonings and the cream or milk. You may not need much salt, but I usually add pepper and 2 teaspoons of sugar, depending on how ripe the tomatoes are.

SALMON AND TARRAGON MOUSSE

TIME NEEDED 30 mins
+CHILLING

SERVES 6 PEOPLE

Ingredients

3 level teaspoons (15 ml) gelatine

1 chicken stock cube

1 oz (25 g) onion skinned and finely chopped

1 garlic skinned and crushed

1 tablespoon chopped fresh tarragon or ½ tablespoon dried

salt and freshly ground pepper

7½oz (213 g) can salmon, drained and coarsely flaked, bones removed

4 teaspoons (60 ml) Greek yoghurt or whipped fresh cream

cucumber, tarragon, watercress and lemon to garnish

Instructions

Preparation

Make up the stock cube with ½ pint (300 ml) warm water, sprinkle the gelatine into this and stand the stock over a pan of hot water to dissolve the gelatine.

Pour into a food processor and add all the remaining ingredients except the yoghurt or cream and garnishes, and process until the mixture is smooth. Alternatively mix together by hand until smooth. Leave to cool in a bowl until just starting to set. Add the yoghurt or whipped cream into the setting salmon mixture. Turn the mousse into a dampened 1 pint (600 ml) ring mould, cover with cling film and chill until set.

Presentation

Garnish with slices of cucumber and lemon around the base, watercress and fresh tarragon in centre. Serve with melba toast or a colourful salad.

TWO GREEK DIPS
TZATZIKI (Yoghurt and cucumber)

Ingredients

1 tablespoon olive oil

1 teaspoon lemon juice

1 clove garlic, crushed

¼ pint (150 ml) plain yoghurt

4 inch (10 cm) piece cucumber, peeled and finely chopped

1 tablespoon chopped mint

salt and freshly ground pepper

Instructions

Preparation

Mix the oil and lemon juice and stir in the garlic. Gradually beat in the yoghurt. Stir in the cucumber and mint and season with salt and pepper. Chill slightly before serving.

Presentation

These can be eaten as a starter, or with drinks as the guests arrive. They are also perfect as part of a summer picnic. Try serving them with triangles of pitta bread warmed gently in the oven, or scooped up on corn chips.

TARAMASALATA

SOUPS & STARTERS

TIME NEEDED 25 mins

SERVES 4 PEOPLE

Ingredients

6 oz (175 g) white bread, crusts removed

2 oz (50 g) salted smoked cod's roe

2 tablespoons lemon juice

1 small onion, chopped

3½ fl oz (90 ml) olive oil

To garnish:

1 tablespoon chopped fresh coriander or parsley

Instructions

Preparation

Soak the bread in a bowl of water for 15 minutes, then drain it and squeeze it almost dry. Make the taramasalata in two batches, putting half the bread, cod's roe, lemon juice, onion and oil into a blender and mixing until smooth and creamy. Repeat with the second batch, then mix both together. The mixing process can be done by hand if you do not have a blender - the flavour should be just as good although the texture may not be quite so smooth.

Presentation

This is a smoked cod's roe dip which can be served with black olive, fingers of warm pitta bread and thin strips of green pepper.

FIERY MOROCCAN CARROT DIP

SOUPS & STARTERS

TIME NEEDED 25 mins

SERVES 6 PEOPLE

Ingredients

1 lb (450 g) carrots

1 teaspoon paprika

a pinch cayenne pepper

1-2 teaspoons cumin powder

¼ teaspoon powder ginger

3 tablespoons wine vinegar

4 tablespoons olive oil

2 cloves garlic, crushed

a small number of black olives

parsley sprigs for garnishing

pitta bread

Instructions

Preparation

Peel or scrub the carrots, and chop into chunks.
Simmer in salt water until soft, and then drain.

Cooking

Mash with a potato masher or fork, or blend in a food
processor for a few seconds. Add the other ingredients
slowly and mix well.

Presentation

Garnish with parsley sprigs and olives.

Cut the pitta bread into wedges or long triangles and
use to scoop up the dip.

CHEESE & EGG DISHES

STILTON AND WALNUT PIE

CHEESE & EGG DISHES

TIME NEEDED 1½ hrs

SERVES 8 PEOPLE

Ingredients

Pastry:
12 oz (350 g) flour
6 oz (175 g) butter or margarine

Filling:
2 eggs, or 3 if you egg glaze
12 oz (350 g) cream cheese
small bunch parsley, chopped
6 oz (175 g) Stilton cheese with rind removed
6 oz (175 g) walnuts, chopped
small onion, finely chopped
salt and pepper
a little oil for frying

For decoration: sticks of celery, watercress amd 1-2 apples, sliced

The amounts given here allow generous slices for 8 people, but it also keeps well for several days in the fridge. It looks attractive served with pieces of celery, watercress and apple (delay cutting the apple until the last minute or sprinkle with lemon juice as it tends to discolour quickly).

STILTON AND WALNUT PIE

Instructions

Preparation

Make the pastry by rubbing the butter into the flour - you may have a machine that will do this. Add just enough cold water to bind it, then cover the pastry and leave to chill in the fridge while you prepare the filling. Beat 2 eggs together; peel and finely chop the onion and fry gently in a little oil until just softened. Chop the parsley and mix the eggs, cream cheese and parsley together, beating until smooth - this can be done in a food processor. Add the fried onion, chopped walnuts and grated or crumbled Stilton. Season to taste; remember that Stilton is a very salty cheese - you may only need pepper and a very little salt.

Grease or line a 9 inch (23 cm) round deepish pie dish or loose-bottomed quiche baking tin. Roll out half the pastry and use to line the base and side, trimming to fit. Spread the cheesy filling on this, smoothing level, then roll out the rest of the pastry to make a lid. Cover the pie, sealing the edges with a little water if you wish, and use the pastry trimmings to make little leaf shapes to decorate the top of the pie. These can be fixed in place with a little beaten egg; the top of the pie can be brushed with the rest of the beaten egg to give an attractive glazed finish.

Cooking

Bake for 45 minutes at gas mark 5, 375°F (190°C) and allow to cool before lifting out of the tin.

ROSEMARY CHEESE SLICES

CHEESE & EGG DISHES

TIME NEEDED 45 mins

MAKES ABOUT 18

Ingredients

2 oz (50 g) butter
5 oz (150 g) oat flakes, or medium oatmeal
6 oz (175 g) Cheddar cheese, grated
I egg
I dessertspoon chopped fresh rosemary
a pinch of salt

This savoury snack is popular ar teatime for those who don't have a sweet tooth.

Instructions

Preparation

Melt the butter in a small pan. Beat the egg in a medium-sized mixing bowl and add all the other ingredients - the melted butter should enable you to bind these together into a stiff dough. Press this out in a greased 8 inch, square baking tin, and make the top smooth.

Cooking

Bake for 30-40 minutes at gas mark 4, 350°F (180°C) until lightly browned and crisp. Leave to cool for a few minutes before cutting into slices.

CRUNCHY MACARONI

Ingredients

2 small or 1 large onion
14 oz (400 g) tin tomatoes
10 oz (280 g) grated cheese
8 oz (250 g) packet quick macaroni
2 tablespoons breadcrumbs
salt and pepper to taste

It may be cheap and cheerful, but this macaroni cheese recipe is one with a difference - you don't have to go to all the bother of making a cheese sauce, just bung it all in the oven.

Instructions

Preparation

Mix the breadcrumbs with 2 oz (50 g) of the grated cheese, and set this mixture aside for the topping. Mash up the tinned tomatoes with 2 tablespoons of water to give extra liquid, season to taste and add the finely chopped onion - or you could whizz up the tomatoes, onion, water and seasoning together in a food processor. Put half the macaroni in a deepish casserole dish and sprinkle half of the grated cheese on top. Spread half the tomato mixture over this and scatter the rest of the macaroni on top. Continue in layers finishing off with a topping of the cheese and breadcrumb mixture.

Cooking

Bake in a fairly low oven, gas mark 3, 325°F (170°C), for 1 hour until the macaroni is cooked. This dish is an ideal one to come home to if you're planning to go out, as it will wait happily in a warm oven until you get home.

NUT LOAF WITH
CHEESE & TOMATO LAYER

CHEESE & EGG DISHES

TIME NEEDED 40 mins

SERVES 4 - 6 PEOPLE

Ingredients

1 medium sized onion, chopped

1 oz (25 g) butter or margarine

8 oz (225 g) chopped mixed nuts

4 oz (100 g) wholemeal bread

4 tablespoons (60 ml) vegetable stock or water

2 teaspoons yeast extract

1 teaspoon mixed herbs

salt and pepper to taste

2 tomatoes, sliced

2 oz (50 g) grated cheese

to garnish:

slices of tomato and cucumber

Instructions

Preparation

Chop the onion and sauté in the butter until transparent. Grind the nuts and bread together in a food processor until quite fine. Heat the stock and yeast extract together to boiling point, then combine all the ingredients and mix well. The mixture will be quite soft. Lightly grease a 1 lb (500 g) loaf tin and line with a strip of baking parchment. Press half the mixture into the prepared loaf tin and cover with the 2 sliced tomatoes and the grated cheese; top with the remaining mixture.

Cooking

Level the surface and bake at gas mark 4, 350°F (180°C) for 30 minutes until golden brown.

Presentation

Garnish with slices of tomato and cucumber.

YORKSHIRE LUNCH

CHEESE & EGG DISHES

Ingredients

1 egg
4 oz (110 g) plain flour
½ pint (275 ml) milk
½ teaspoon salt
4 oz (110 g) Cheddar cheese
½ an onion, chopped
6 oz (175 g) cooked potato
1 dessertspoon oil

Anyone who likes toad-in-the-hole will probably enjoy this quick and cheap vegetarian version. It makes a family meal from leftovers and bits most people have in.

TIME NEEDED 45 mins

SERVES 4 PEOPLE

Instructions

Preparation

Make the batter by beating the egg, milk, flour and salt together, then leave to stand while you are getting the other ingredients ready. Peel and roughly chop the onion, chop the cooked potato into chunks. Put the oil into a large roasting tin, add the onion and potato pieces and mix around.

Cooking

Put into a hot oven, gas mark 7, 425°F (220°C), for 5-10 minutes to heat thoroughly and crisp up the onion. Meanwhile, cut the cheese into large cubes and have the batter ready to hand. As soon as you take the roasting tin out of the oven (the oil must be hot when you add the batter), quickly sprinkle in the cheese chunks and pour the batter over everything. Put the tin back in the hot oven and cook for 20-25 minutes, when it should be risen and golden brown.

CHEESE TRIANGLES

CHEESE & EGG DISHES

TIME NEEDED 1 hr

MAKES ABOUT 24

Ingredients

6 oz (175 g) ricotta or cottage cheese

6 oz (175 g) feta or Wensleydale cheese

2 oz (50 g) kefalotiri or parmesan cheese, grated

2 eggs, lightly beaten

2 tablespoons chopped parsley

a pinch of grated nutmeg

freshly ground pepper

1 ½ oz (40 g) filo pastry

water for sprinkling

These are Greek pastries, otherwise known as tiropitakia, but you can use English cheeses if the traditional Greek ones are difficult to find.

CHEESE TRIANGLES

Instructions

Preparation

Mix all the cheeses together in a bowl of food processor. Add the eggs and parsley, and season with the nutmeg and pepper. Brush the bottom of a 9 x 7 inch (23 x 18 cm) metal baking dish with melted butter. Cut the sheets of filo pastry to fit the dish and make a layer of 6 sheets, brushing each one with melted butter. Keep the remaining pastry covered with a damp cloth to prevent it drying out. Spread the cheese filling over the pastry, then cover it with another 6 sheets, again brushing each one with melted butter. Mark the top into triangles, cutting through almost to the cheese filling. Sprinkle a little water over the pastry top to prevent it curling at the edges.

Cooking

Bake the pie at gas mark 5, 375°F (190°C) until the top is crisp and brown. Leave to cool slightly and, if it is to be served straight away, cut it into the marked triangles.

Presentation

If you are handing the pastries round at an indoor drinks party, provide plates or paper napkins - they are delightfully crumbly, but very messy.

SWISS FONDUE

Ingredients

1 lb cheese, grated
½ pint (275 ml - about ¼ of a bottle) dry white wine
2 tablespoons kirsch (optional)
1 clove garlic, peeled and cut in two
1 level tablespoon cornflour
black pepper and grated nutmeg to season

Use Gruyère or Gouda cheese; for a more British flavour, you can always use Cheddar. Don't worry if you don't have a fondue set - just put the pan on the table and eat rapidly! It will be so popular the cheese won't have a chance to set.

Instructions

Preparation

Rub the peeled and halved clove of garlic around the inside of your pan, then put the pan on a medium heat and pour in the wine - if you're not using kirsch, save a little wine for mixing the cornflour.

Add the grated cheese to the wine while it is heating, and stir with a wooden spoon until the cheese starts to melt. Mix the cornflour to a smooth paste with the kirsch or a little white wine, add to the cheese mixture, and keep stirring. Season with a little grated nutmeg and black pepper.

Cooking

The fondue is ready when it is thick and smooth and has bubbled for a minute or less - don't allow to boil hard, or for long, as the cheese will go tough and stringy.

POULTRY

GINGER DUCK

TIME NEEDED 30 mins
+MARINADING

SERVES 4 PEOPLE

Ingredients

4 duck breasts

1 tablespoon salt

juice and grated rind of half an orange

1 onion, chopped

2 cloves garlic, crushed

¾ inch (2 cm) piece of fresh root ginger, peeled and finely chopped

¼ pint (150 ml) Hoisin sauce

1 tablespoon dark soy sauce

5 tablespoons yellow bean paste

1 teaspoon five spice powder

2 teaspoons vegetable oil, preferably groundnut

2 tablespoons clear honey

Soy sauce and lemon dip:

3 spring onions, trimmed and sliced diagonally

4 tablespoons soy sauce

juice of 1 lemon

dash of hot pepper sauce

freshly ground black pepper

These kebabs are absolutely delicious and can be served with a soy and lemon dip (the duck can be replaced by chicken if you prefer).

GINGER DUCK

Instructions

Preparation

Rub the skin with salt to make crispier when cooked. Squeeze the fresh orange juice over the duck portions and cut each breast into chunks. Place the onion, garlic and ginger in processor. Blend for a few seconds. Add the Hoisin sauce, dark soy sauce, yellow bean paste, five spice powder, vegetable oil, clear honey and the rest of the juice. Blend until smooth.

Cooking

Place the duck pieces in a shallow container and pour the marinade over them. Stir to ensure that the duck is covered by the sauce; cover and chill for at least 2 hours.

Thread the duck pieces onto bamboo skewers. Preheat the grill and cook for 15 minutes turning regularly and basting with the marinade until crispy. Garnish with orange rind.

To make the soy sauce dip, mix the spring onions with the lemon juice, hot pepper sauce and black pepper.

SESAME CHICKEN

TIME NEEDED 50 mins
+ MARINADING

SERVES 4 PEOPLE

Ingredients

4 large or 8 small chicken thighs
2 level tablespoons sesame seeds

Marinade:
8 tablespoons dark soy sauce
2 tablespoons orange marmalade
1 inch pinch fresh ginger, peeled and grated, or
½ teaspoon ground ginger
1 tablespoon sesame oil
2 cloves garlic, crushed

Instructions

Preparation

Place all the marinade ingredients together in a deep bowl. Skin the chicken thighs and put into the marinade, ensuring that they are well covered. Leave for a minimum of 2 hours, turning at least once.

Cooking

Put the chicken on a rack over a baking tray. Sprinkle with sesame seeds and cook at gas mark 7, 425°F (220°C) for 15 minutes. Baste with any marinade mixture which drips into the base of the tray. Turn the oven down to gas mark 5, 375°F (190°C) and cook for a further 20-30 minutes, when the chicken joints should be thoroughly cooked. This dish is equally good served either hot or cold.

HERBED CHICKEN WITH ORANGE

Ingredients

2 chicken pieces
juice of 1 orange
a little oil for frying
1 teaspoon thyme
1 teaspoon marjoram
salt and pepper

A deliciously tangy dish that is very easy to make - use chicken breasts if you can afford them, or a cheaper joint such as thighs.

Instructions

Preparation

You need to cook this in a flame-proof casserole that has a lid, or in a thick-bottomed small pan. Heat the oil, and brown the chicken pieces on both sides. Squeeze the juice from the orange, and pour over the meat, adding salt and pepper and the chopped fresh herbs.

Cooking

Shake the pan to mix the flavours, cover and leave to simmer gently until the chicken is cooked - the juice will not cover the meat, but it will cook in the steam if you keep the lid on. Turn the chicken pieces once during the cooking time, which will be 20-30 minutes, depending on the size and cut of chicken used.

Test to see if the chicken is cooked by piercing the thickest part of the meat with a knife - if the juices run clear, it is done.

FAJITAS

POULTRY

TIME NEEDED 30 mins
+MARINADING

SERVES 4 PEOPLE

Ingredients

1½ lb (750 g) of skinned chicken breast

Marinade:
juice of 3 limes or 4 small lemons
4 tablespoons freshly chopped coriander
1 green pepper, de-seeded and chopped
salt and pepper
tortillas

These are delicious Mexican tortillas containing strips of chicken which have been soaked in a tangy lime and coriander marinade.

Instructions

Preparation

Cut the meat into strips. Combine the lime or lemon juice, the coriander, green pepper, salt and pepper in a food processor (or mix well by hand, first chopping the green pepper into very small pieces). Pour this marinade over the strips of meat, making sure that they are covered. Allow the meat to marinate for at least 2-3 hours.

Cooking

Cook under a preheated grill, or on a hot barbeque, for 5-10 minutes when the chicken pieces should be cooked. Warm the tortillas under the grill and spread with a little guacamole (see page 27) or add some avocado slices if you prefer a slightly milder taste. Top with slices of vegetable such as pepper and tomato, add the barbequed chicken and roll up the tortillas. Eat immediately!

GUACAMOLE

POULTRY

TIME NEEDED 10 mins

SERVES 4 PEOPLE

Ingredients

1 ripe avocado
juice of ½ a lemon
1 tablespoon olive oil
½ small onion
1 or 2 cloves garlic, crushed
1 tomato, chopped
a dash of tabasco sauce

This Mexican avocado dish provides an unusual accompaniment to the fajitas described on page 26. You can vary its strength by adding more or less garlic, and it also stands very well on its own, perhaps as a dip or part of a salad assortment.

Instructions

Preparation

Remove the flesh of the avocado from the shell and beat all the ingredients together, taking care to add the olive oil gradually. A food processor or liquidiser is useful for making this dish but it can be made by hand if you use some elbow grease and don't mind a slightly coarser texture.

SWEDISH CHICKEN SALAD

Ingredients

1 medium-large roasting chicken

1 green dessert apple

1 red dessert apple

2 bananas

lemon juice

¼ pint (150 ml) whipping cream or Greek yoghurt

7 fl oz (200 ml) mayonnaise

1 teaspoon curry powder

salt and pepper

watercress to garnish

Instructions

Cooking

Roast the chicken (allowing 20 minutes for every 1 lb (450 g) and 20 minutes over); let it cool and cut the meat into slices, then thin strips. Slice the apples and bananas thinly, and coat in lemon juice to prevent discolouration. If you are using cream, whip it to the same consistency as mayonnaise. Combine cream or yoghurt with mayonnaise, carefully blend in the curry powder and then fold in chicken, and fruit and season according to taste.

Presentation

Garnish with watercress.

BUTTERED CHICKEN
WITH SPICED NUT SAUCE

POULTRY

TIME NEEDED 40 mins

SERVES 6 PEOPLE

Ingredients

3 oz (75 g) unsalted butter

3 oz (75 g) cashew nuts

6 chicken breast fillets

1 large onion, chopped

2 cloves garlic, chopped

1 tablespoon grated fresh ginger

seeds from 4 green cardomom pods, crushed

¼ pint (150 ml) double cream

salt and black pepper

1 tablespoon garam marsala

Instructions

Preparation

Melt half the butter in a pan, add 1 oz (25 g) of the cashew nuts and fry until pale gold, then remove from the pan.

Cooking

Toss the chicken breasts in flour and fry over a medium heat for about 8-10 minutes until cooked through. Remove from the pan and set aside. Meanwhile, melt the remaining butter and fry the onion, garlic and ginger for about 5 minutes until the onion is soft. Stir in the cardomom seeds and the remaining cashew nuts, keeping a few back for decoration. Place in a food processor or blender and purée to a smooth paste. Add the cream, seasoning and garam marsala. Return the sauce to the pan, add the chicken and heat thoroughly. Serve scattered with lightly-fried cashew nuts.

NASI GORENG

Ingredients

8 oz (225 g) rice or Indonesian or Chinese noodles

12 fl oz (425 ml) chicken stock

1 large onion, chopped

1 clove garlic, crushed

½ green pepper, seeded and chopped

2 oz (50 g) button mushrooms

6 oz (150 g) chicken breast, skinned and sliced

4 oz (110 g) peeled, cooked prawns

2 oz (50 g) shelled, unsalted peanuts

2 oz (50 g) frozen peas

2 tablespoons soy sauce

1 tablespoon oyster sauce

1 dessertspoon curry powder

a little oil for cooking, preferably groundnut

Instructions

Preparation

Cook the noodles or rice in the chicken stock until soft
- this should take about 7-10 minutes. Cut the chicken
into small pieces and marinade in a mixture of the
oyster and soy sauce for 2 hours or more.

Cooking

Sauté the chicken in the oil in a wok or large frying pan
for about 2 minutes. Remove the chicken onto a plate.
Add the garlic, chopped onion, pepper and mushrooms
to the wok and stir fry for approximately 3 minutes.
Add the curry powder and return the chicken pieces to
the wok and add the peas, prawns and cooked noodles.
Stir fry until heated thoroughly - about 2 minutes.

TASTY TURKEY

Ingredients

4 turkey fillets (escalopes)
1½ oz (40 g) butter
1 tablespoon oil, preferably olive or sunflower
1 onion, sliced
1 red pepper, de-seeded and thinly sliced
1 tablespoon plain flour
7 fl oz (200 ml) lager or pale ale
¼ pint (150 ml) chicken stock
½ teaspoon dried mixed herbs
1 teaspoon sugar
4 tablespoons single cream
salt and pepper

Instructions

Preparation

Slice the turkey fillets in half through the centre with a sharp knife so that you have 8 thin slices. Heat the butter and oil in a large pan until the butter is melted. Season each slice of turkey with salt and pepper, and fry the slices, a few at a time depending on how many you can fit in the pan, for about 3 minutes on each side until they are golden brown. Keep the slices warm in a low oven. Peel and slice the onion, de-seed and thinly slice the green pepper, and fry them until softened in the same oil that you used to cook the turkey.

Cooking

Stir in the flour and cook for a minute, then gradually add the lager and stock, mixing all the time over a low heat. Bring to the boil, stirring continuously; add the herbs and sugar. Put the turkey slices into this sauce, and simmer until tender - about 10 minutes. Take off the heat and stir in the cream. Taste and season as required.

PASTA AL POLLO

POULTRY

TIME NEEDED 35 mins

SERVES 3 PEOPLE

Ingredients

12 oz (350 g) pasta
2 chicken breast fillets
8 oz (225 g) mushrooms, sliced
1 clove garlic, crushed
7 fl oz (200 ml) double cream
2 tablespoons olive oil
to garnish: freshly chopped parsley

This Italian pasta dish combines chicken and mushrooms in a creamy sauce – just the thing for a quick but impressive supper dish.

Instructions

Preparation

Bring a large pan of salted water to the boil and add the pasta. Leave to cook, stirring occasionally, for about 10-12 minutes until soft but still chewy. Meanwhile, cut the chicken into small pieces and fry in the oil until just golden. Remove from the pan and set aside.

Sauté the garlic for a few seconds in the oil left over from the chicken. Add the sliced mushrooms and fry gently until soft. Return the chicken pieces to the pan, and mix gently with the mushrooms until thoroughly heated. Take off the heat and leave to cool for a few seconds while you drain the pasta.

Add the cream to the chicken mixture, stir well to form a thick sauce and serve on top of the pasta, decorating with some freshly chopped parsley.

MEAT

MINTED MEATBALLS

LAMB OR BEEF

TIME NEEDED 45 mins

SERVES 4 PEOPLE

Ingredients

1¼ lb (560 g) minced lamb or beef
1 tablespoon cooking oil
1 small onion, chopped
3 tablespoons chopped parsley
2 tablespoons chopped mint
salt and pepper to taste

If you have ever been on holiday to Greece, you may remember eating mint in meat dishes. This is my own version of one of them.

Instructions

Preparation

Heat the oil in a frying pan, and fry the chopped onion until soft. Put the minced meat into a large bowl, add the salt and pepper and the chopped mint and parsley; tip in the onion and mix well together.

Cooking

The mixture should be firm enough to make into small balls which can then be baked in a moderate oven, gas mark 4, 350°F (180°C), on a greased baking tray for 30 minutes. Turn once halfway through the cooking time.

Presentation

Serve with a crisp salad and either rice or pitta bread - you could add some of the tzatziki (page 8) for an extra Greek touch.

SALSA VERDE

Ingredients

1 egg yolk
1 dessertspoon Dijon or French mustard
1 heaped teaspoon sugar
salt and pepper
2 cloves garlic, crushed
½ a small onion, chopped
1½ oz (40 g) chopped mixed fresh herbs
    I suggest parsley, chives and tarragon
3 tablespoons white wine vinegar
¼ pint (150 ml) olive oil
2 hard-boiled eggs

This Italian sauce can be served as an accompaniment to cold meat, or with new potatoes and crisp, green vegetables. The amounts given here are enough for 6 to go with a starter, so if you are cooking for fewer, plan things so that you can have some left over for the next day's meal.

Instructions

Preparation

If you are making this without a food processor, start with the egg yolk, beating it in a bowl; then add the ingredients in the order given, beating well between each addition, adding the oil in stages and chopping the hard-boiled eggs as small as you can before adding them to the sauce. If you have a food processor, you can put the whole lot in at once and blend.

CASSOULET

Ingredients

1 lb (450 g) sausage, preferably Cumberland
½ lb (350 g) bacon, rind removed
1 large onion, chopped
a little oil for frying
2 tins beans, 14 oz (400 g) size, I suggest red kidney beans
and flageolets or cannellini
garlic to taste
between a third and a half of a tube of tomato purée

There are many versions of this French peasant dish, and I don't care who says mine isn't authentic, everyone seems to like it and it's a family favourite. Both my daughters make this if they're feeding a gang of friends as it will happily keep warm without spoiling if someone is late. Gilly uses one clove of garlic, I use 2, and Sophie puts in 3, so please yourself.

Instructions

Cooking

Grill or bake the sausage, turning at least once until it is well browned. Fry the peeled and chopped onion in the oil in a large pan or flameproof casserole. Add the garlic, then the bacon, chopped into pieces.

Continue to stir until the onion has softened and the bacon looks nearly done, then drain and rinse the tinned beans and add to the pan with the tomato purée and a little pepper; don't add salt yet - you may not need it as bacon is usually so salty. Add enough hot water to just cover the sausage mixture, stir gently to mix the tomato purée in but not break up the beans and leave to simmer gently for about 15 minutes for the flavours to blend. Taste and adjust seasoning to please.

SPARE RIB CHOPS
WITH THYME

PORK

TIME NEEDED 1½ hrs

SERVES 2 PEOPLE

Ingredients

1 small onion, cut into rings
1 crisp eating apple
2 teaspoons chopped thyme
1 oz (25 g) sultanas
1 clove garlic, crushed
little oil for frying
½ pint (275 g) dry cider, or
¼ pint (150 ml) apple juice and ¼ pint (150 ml) water

Instructions

Cooking

Use a flame-proof casserole if you have one, otherwise start cooking in a frying pan then change to a lidded casserole for the oven. Fry the chops in the oil until nicely browned on each side, then add the onion, sliced into rings. Add the garlic, mix over the heat, then core the apple and add in thick slices. Season with salt and pepper, add the sultanas, thyme and cider, or the apple juice and water to make half a pint of liquid. Put the lid on, and cook in a moderate oven, gas mark 4, 350°F (180°C) for about three quarters of an hour or until the meat is tender.

SAUTÉED PORK
IN A CITRUS SAUCE

PORK

TIME NEEDED 40 mins

SERVES 2 PEOPLE

Ingredients

8 oz (225 g) pork tenderloin
seasoned flour
1 medium orange
1 medium grapefruit
4 tablespoons (60 ml) dry white wine
1 level tablespoon chopped fresh coriander
1 tablespoon oil
1 oz (25 g) butter
a pinch of paprika
6 tablespoons (90 ml) double cream
salt and pepper
to garnish: orange and grapefruit slices and fresh coriander

Instructions

Preparation

Cut the pork tenderloin across into ¼ inch (5 mm) slices. Place the slices between two sheets of damp greaseproof paper or cling film and, using a rolling pin, flatten into thin pieces. Dip these into the seasoned flour. Put 2 tablespoons each of orange and grapefruit juice into a small saucepan, add the dry white wine and fresh coriander and boil until reduced by half.

Cooking

Meanwhile, heat the oil with the butter in a medium-sized frying pan and fry the pork slices briskly for 2 minutes on each side or until cooked through. Add the juice mixture, the paprika and the cream. Simmer gently for 1-2 minutes until thoroughly heated. Season to taste.

Presentation

Serve with new potatoes and courgettes or broccoli.

PORK HONGROISE

TIME NEEDED 1½ hrs

SERVES 4 PEOPLE

Ingredients

1 lb (500 g) trimmed pork pieces
14 oz (400 g) tin chopped tomatoes
1 green pepper, de-seeded and sliced into strips
1 teaspoon paprika
2 oz (50 g) mushrooms
1 tablespoon tomato purée
1 lemon
1 dessertspoon Worcester sauce
2 tablespoons natural yoghurt or sour cream
1 onion
salt and pepper
parsley for garnish
¼ pint (150 ml) water

Instructions

Preparation

Lightly fry the pork pieces with the paprika and onion.
Add the sliced green pepper, trimmed mushrooms,
seasoning, tinned tomatoes, purée and the Worcester
sauce.

Cooking

Turn into a casserole dish, stir in the water and cook
gently either in the oven at gas mark 4-5, 350°F
(180°C) or on a hob for approximately 40 minutes until
the pork is tender.

Presentation

Just before serving pour natural yoghurt or sour cream
down the centre of the casserole. Sprinkle lightly with a
little paprika. Garnish with lemon and parsley.

TANDOORI BEEF KEBABS

TIME NEEDED 40 mins

SERVES 4 PEOPLE

Ingredients

1 lb (450 g) lean minced beef
1 teaspoon paprika
1 crushed clove garlic
1 inch (2.5 cm) piece fresh ginger root, peeled and
chopped
½ teaspoon ground coriander
1 tablespoon tandoori spice
a pinch chilli powder
salt and pepper
1 egg
2 tablespoons lemon juice

Yoghurt sauce:
5 oz (150 g) carton natural yoghurt
4 chopped mint leaves
½ teaspoon clear honey
1 clove garlic, crushed
1½ teaspoons chopped coriander leaves
pinch chilli powder
½ teaspoon paprika

To garnish: chopped coriander leaves, lemon wedges

These are wonderfully colourful and a little different to serve
at a barbeque or dinner party. The minced beef makes
them quite economical to make.

TANDOORI BEEF KEBABS

Instructions

Preparation

Place the minced meat in a large bowl. Add the garlic, ginger, tandoori spice, coriander, chilli powder, salt, pepper, and half of the paprika, and beat in the egg. Alternatively, combine all the ingredients together in a food processor if you have one. Divide the mixture into 8 portions and mould into 2 long thin sausage shapes on each of 4 oiled skewers.

Yoghurt sauce: to make the yoghurt sauce, combine all the ingredients, except for the paprika, in a small serving bowl; sprinkle the paprika over the top.

Cooking

Cook the kebabs on a hot barbeque or under a preheated grill for 10-15 minutes turning frequently until browned. Serve sprinkled with lemon juice and the remaining paprika.

Presentation

Serve on a bed of golden coloured rice with wedges of lemon and garnished with coriander leaves. The yoghurt sauce can be served separately.

HOT AND NUTTY PORK KEBABS

Ingredients

1½ lb (750 g) boneless pork shoulder steak

2 cloves garlic crushed

1 green chilli, deseeded and finely chopped

2 teaspoon tamarind concentrate or 4 teaspoons lemon juice

3 tablespoons groundnut or sunflower oil

1 level tablespoon black treacle

1 level tablespoon soy sauce

1 rounded teaspoon ground coriander

2 medium sized red peppers

3 tablespoons smooth peanut butter

½ pint (150 ml) water

These kebabs are Indonesian in origin. They are delicious served hot or cold with a bowl of rice and a yoghurt sauce. The chicken can be substituted for pork.

(continued)

(Opposite) Fiery Moroccan carrot dip (page 10) served with pitta bread and crudités, and carrot ring with walnuts (page 71)

(Overleaf) Leek and mushroom filo parcels (page 74), melon with stilton and watercress sauce (page 2) and salmon and tarragon mousse (page 7) served with a crisp salad of mixed lettuce leaves

HOT AND NUTTY PORK KEBABS

Instructions (continued)

Preparation

Cut the pork or chicken into 1 inch (2.5 cm) cubes and put these into a bowl. Take care when preparing chillis as some people find the juice from them burns on the skin. I find it best to cut them open under running water and remove the seeds. Chop the garlic and chillis together very finely. Prepare the paste by mixing together in a smaller bowl the peanut butter, tamarind concentrate or lemon juice, oil, treacle, soy sauce, coriander, chopped chilli, water and garlic. Alternatively combine all these ingredients together in a food processor. Add this paste to the pork or chicken ensuring that the meat is covered with the paste. Leave to stand for at least a couple of hours.

Cooking

After discarding the seeds from the peppers, cut them into wedges. Thread the pork and pepper onto oiled skewers. Cook the kebabs on a hot barbeque or under a preheated grill until tender.

Presentation

Serve either hot or cold with rice and a yoghurt sauce

(Overleaf) Spiced apple soup (page 3) and nasi goreng (page 30)

(Opposite) Ratatouille (page 63) and pork hongroise (page 39), served with a mixture of long grain and wild rice

SWEET AND SOUR BACON CHOPS

PORK

TIME NEEDED 35 mins

SERVES 4 PEOPLE

Ingredients

4 bacon chops

8 oz (225 g) tin pineapple slices

½ onion, chopped

1 tablespoon chopped parsley

1 heaped teaspoon cornflour

2 teaspoons soy sauce

You can cook this under a grill; if your grill pan can also be put on top of the stove use it to finish off the sauce.

Instructions

Cooking

Put the slices of onion in a grill pan, lay the bacon chops on top, and cook under the grill until the chops look done and nicely browned - about 15 minutes, turning them once. Take out the chops and keep warm.

Reserving the liquid, drain the pineapple slices and add them to the onion which will have cooked in the juices coming from the meat. Mix together and heat thoroughly, either under the grill or by frying gently on top of the cooker. Blend the cornflour into a smooth paste with a little of the pineapple juice, then add the rest of the juice, half a teacup of water and the chopped parsley. Add the soy sauce and season with a little pepper but *not* salt as there will be plenty of salt in the cooking juices that have come from the bacon. Pour this liquid into the grill/frying pan containing the onion and pineapple, and stir continuously over the heat until the sauce thickens.

Presentation

Pour over the bacon chops which can be served with rice.

CHEESE AND TOMATO HAMBURGERS

LAMB OR BEEF

TIME NEEDED 25 mins

SERVES (SEE RECIPE)

Ingredients

2 oz (50 g) fresh white breadcrumbs

1¼ lb (560 g) finely minced lean beef or lamb

1 onion, finely chopped

½ teaspoon dried basil or 1 teaspoon fresh basil chopped

½ teaspoon finely grated lemon rind

1 oz (25 g) Cheddar cheese grated

1 tablespoon tomato purée or ketchup

salt and pepper

vegetable oil

These are a great favourite with the children. Try serving them topped with corn relish.

Instructions

Preparation

Put all the ingredients except the oil in a bowl or a food processor and mix thoroughly.

Using floured hands, divide the mixture into 10 equal portions, knead lightly and shape into burgers. Cover and refrigerate for up to 12 hours until ready to cook.

Cooking

Brush the burgers with oil and cook on a hot barbeque or under a hot grill for 5 minutes. Turn and brush the burgers again with oil and cook for further 5-8 minutes or until they are cooked.

Presentation

Serve them in a roll topped with corn relish. These amounts will serve 10 small children or 4-5 adults.

STUFFED BREAST OF LAMB

LAMB

TIME NEEDED 25 mins
+ROASTING

SERVES 4 PEOPLE

Ingredients

I large or 2 small breasts of lamb, boned.

These are often sold boned out ready to roll, but if not, any butcher will do it for you. They are smaller earlier in the season.

For the stuffing:
4 oz (I I0 g) brown bread
4 oz (I I0 g) no-soak dried apricots
I small onion, quartered
I small bunch parsley, finely chopped
I egg
salt and pepper
You will also need some string.

Here is a recipe for people who are stunned by the cost of a family roast for Sunday lunch. It gives you the impression of having a large joint to carve, but is very cheap, and there are no bones to hinder the carver.

Instructions

Preparation

Tear the break into chunks. Peel and quarter the onion and put it into a food processor with the bread, apricots and parsley and process for a few seconds until all large chunks have broken down.

STUFFED BREAST OF LAMB

Instructions

Preparation

If you don't have a food processor, you will have to chop the onion, parsley and apricots finely, make the bread into crumbs and mix together. Season the mixture to taste, add the beaten egg and mix with a fork to bind the crumbs together.

Lay the breast of lamb skin side down, and spread with the stuffing; then roll up like a swiss roll. If you are using 2 smaller breasts, form the stuffing into a fat sausage shape down the middle of one breast, skin side down, and place the other, skin side up, over the top. Form into a roll that encloses the stuffing and tie firmly together with lots of string - you can cut this off after the lamb is cooked before bringing it to the table.

Cooking

Weigh the roll you have made, and roast it on a rack in a roasting tin at gas mark 7, 425°F (220°C) for 25 minutes per 1 lb (450 g) and 25 minutes over.

SMOOTH PÂTÉ

SOUPS & STARTERS

TIME NEEDED 30 mins
+CHILLING

SERVES 4 PEOPLE

Ingredients

1 lb (450 g) chicken or turkey livers
2 or 3 cloves garlic, crushed
1 large or 2 small onions
1 tablespoon oil, preferably olive
3 oz (75 g) butter
1 sherry glass measure of sherry or brandy

It works out much cheaper to make your own pâté than to buy it. This recipe uses much less fat than most, and it makes quite a soft pâté. Chicken or turkey livers can be bought frozen in most supermarkets.

Instructions

Preparation

Melt the butter in a large frying pan with the oil, add the crushed garlic and fry for a few seconds before adding the chopped onion. Fry together until the onion starts to go soft, then add the livers, chopped into pieces if they are large. Fry gently, turning frequently, until they are done - about 10 minutes. The livers can be pinkish in the middle, but not red or bloody.

Presentation

Season generously with salt and pepper, take off the heat and add the sherry or brandy. Put through a blender or food processor, then pour into small pots and chill well - preferably overnight - before serving. This recipe makes several small pots, so I make a batch and freeze it, and there's always something my husband can find to eat when I'm away!

FISH & SEAFOOD

SALMON STEAK PARCELS

FISH & SEAFOOD

TIME NEEDED 25 mins

SERVES (SEE RECIPE)

Ingredients

for each person:
1 salmon steak
¼ bulb fennel, finely chopped
2 mushrooms, chopped
salt and pepper
a little lemon juice

Instructions

Preparation

Chop the mushrooms and fennel finely and mix together; put the vegetable mixture into the middle of a piece of foil about 14 inches square and place the salmon steak on top of this. Add a squeeze of lemon juice and some seasoning, then wrap the foil up to form a parcel.

Cooking

Bake in the oven at gas mark 5, 375°F (190°C) for 15 minutes.

Presentation

Serve with new potatoes and crisp green vegetables.

FISH SALAD

Ingredients

the salad:
1 small tin tuna fish in brine or 2 small smoked mackerel
fillets
1 apple, cored and chopped
2 inch (5 cm) piece of cucumber, diced
2 tomatoes, chopped

for the dressing:
small carton low-fat yoghurt
1 tablespoon chopped parsley
1 teaspoon of lemon juice or ½ teaspoon horseradish sauce

You can make this with peppered smoked fillets of
mackerel, or with tuna fish if you prefer.

Instructions

Preparation

Drain and flake the tuna fish, or flake the mackerel and discard the skin. Mix the fish with the apple, cucumber, and tomatoes.

Presentation

Combine the dressing ingredients and mix with the salad; serve on a bed of lettuce with fresh bread.

ROLLED FISH WITH
FENNEL AND ORANGE

FISH & SEAFOOD

TIME NEEDED 30 mins

SERVES 4 PEOPLE

Ingredients

2 large or 4 small fillets of plaice
1 orange
1 bulb fennel
salt and pepper

Instructions

Preparation

Skin the fish - the fishmonger may do this for you - and if you are using 2 large fillets, cut each in half lengthways. Trim the leaves from the fennel bulb and lay them on the fish pieces. Chop or grate the rest of the fennel bulb and place in a shallow, ovenproof dish.

Peel the orange and cut into chunks, removing all pips and pith. Put the orange, with any juice that ran while you were cutting it, on top of the fennel. Roll the pieces of fish around the fennel leaves and place on top of the orange.

Cooking

Season with salt and pepper, then either put a lid on the dish or cover with foil. Bake in a fairly hot oven, gas mark 6, 400°F (200°C), for 20 minutes.

CREOLE SAUCE

THIS IS IDEAL FOR FISH RECIPES.

SAUCE

TIME NEEDED 35 mins

SERVES 3 - 4 PEOPLE

Ingredients

I large onion, peeled and chopped

I tablespoon oil

I green pepper, cored, seeded and finely chopped

I 4 oz can chopped tomatoes

I red pepper, cored, seeded and chopped

a large pinch of dry mustard

I teaspoon sugar

I tablespoon lemon juice

freshly ground pepper

I tablespoon chopped fresh parsley

Instructions

Cooking

Gently cook the onions in hot oil until they are soft but not brown; add the remaining ingredients (all except the parsley). Simmer for 20 minutes until the sauce is cooked and slightly thickened.

Presentation

Add the chopped parsley just before serving.

COCONUT PRAWNS

FISH & SEAFOOD

TIME NEEDED 45 mins
+MARINADING

SERVES 4 PEOPLE

Ingredients

24 large peeled prawns

3 oz (75 g) creamed coconut

1 clove garlic, crushed

½ teaspoon ground cumin

¼ teaspoon chilli powder

1 tablespoon chopped fresh coriander

1 tablespoon lemon or lime juice

5 oz (125 g) pot of plain yoghurt

4 bamboo skewers

The creamed coconut and the fresh coriander give this recipe a wonderful oriental flavour.

Instructions

Preparation

Add ¼ pint (150 ml) of hot water to the creamed coconut and blend until smooth, either by hand or in a food processor. Add the coriander, garlic, cumin, chilli powder and lemon or lime juice. Blend until smooth.

Place the prawns in a shallow dish. Add the coconut paste and stir to coat well. Cover and chill for 2 hours.

Thread 2 prawns onto a bamboo skewer so that they interlock with each other, and repeat until there are 6 prawns on each skewer.

COCONUT PRAWNS

Instructions

Cooking

Place under a pre-heated grill and cook for 5 minutes on each side until the prawns are pink and the marinade begins to brown.

Add the yoghurt to the remaining marinade and place in a saucepan; bring to the boil and simmer until it is fairly thick.

Presentation

Serve the prawns with rice and a generous helping of the sauce.

HALIBUT STEAK
WITH ROSEMARY

Ingredients

1 halibut steak, ½ lb (225 g) in weight
1 oz (25 g) finely chopped shallot or onion
1 medium tomato
1 teaspoon chopped fresh rosemary
a little oil
salt and pepper

Instructions

Preparation

Take a piece of baking foil big enough to wrap your piece of fish in a parcel, and brush with a little oil. Season one side of the fish, and lay it seasoned side down on the foil. Put the chopped onion or shallot on top of the fish, and the chopped tomato on top of this - you can skin the tomato if you prefer. Add the rosemary and a little more salt and pepper, then parcel up the whole and put in a baking tray.

Cooking

Cook in the oven at gas mark 4, 350°F (180°C) for a little less than 30 minutes, or until the fish is cooked.

SEAFOOD AND
PINEAPPLE CREOLE

FISH & SEAFOOD

TIME NEEDED 30 mins

SERVES 4 PEOPLE

Ingredients

9 oz (250 g) white fish, skinned, boned and cut into bite-sized pieces

2 tablespoons (30 ml) olive oil

2 spring onions, chopped

2 large cloves garlic, chopped

9 oz (250 g) large prawns, cooked and peeled

salt and pepper

1 star anise

½ teaspoon ground turmeric

1 bay leaf

2 teaspoons grated orange zest

¼ teaspoon cayenne pepper

¼ pint (275 ml) boiling water

6 teaspoons cornflour

3 tablespoons dry sherry

2 tablespoons soy sauce

9 oz (250 g) fresh or canned unsweetened pineapple chunks

This recipe can be cooked in the microwave or on the hob.

Instructions

Cooking

Combine the fish, oil, spring onions and garlic in a large casserole, either sauté for 5 minutes or microwave on high for 2 minutes. Stir in the prawns, salt, pepper, star anise, turmeric, bay leaf, orange zest and cayenne pepper. Stir in the boiling water and simmer gently for 5 minutes or microwave on high for 2 minutes. Blend the cornflour, sherry and soy sauce. Stir into the casserole mixture, simmer for 3-4 minutes until the liquid starts to thicken, or microwave on high for 2-3 minutes stirring once every minute until the sauce thickens. Stir in the pineapple and heat gently. Serve with boiled rice.

10 MINUTE SUPPER

FISH & SEAFOOD

TIME NEEDED 10 mins

SERVES 2 PEOPLE

Ingredients

6 oz (175 g) defrosted frozen, or shelled fresh prawns

½ an onion

6-8 oz (175-225 g) ribbon pasta (tagliatelle)

1 green pepper, de-seeded and chopped

1 small tin sweetcorn

1 clove garlic, crushed

small amount chopped parsley

salt and pepper

½ carton Greek yoghurt (8 oz, 225 g size)

a little oil or butter for frying

This is my suggestion for a really quick and easy supper dish for Richard and Judy, who wanted something either of them could make while the other was settling the children into bed.

Instructions

Preparation

First boil some water in the kettle, pour into a pan, add a generous pinch of salt and when the water has come to the boil once again, add the pasta - it should be done in 8-10 minutes. Test by tasting a small piece - when ready it should be chewy but not too soft or soggy.

10 MINUTE SUPPER

Instructions

Cooking

While the pasta is cooking, melt a little butter or oil in a frying pan and gently sauté the peeled and chopped onion together with the crushed garlic - for extra speed, use an inch of garlic paste from a tube.
After 2 minutes, add the de-seeded and chopped green pepper, continue frying and stirring for 2 minutes longer, then add the prawns and drained sweetcorn.

Presentation

Heat thoroughly for a few seconds, then take off the heat; add the chopped parsley, salt and pepper to taste, and the yoghurt. Stir together until the yoghurt has coated the other ingredients to form a thick sauce. By this time, the pasta should be cooked so drain it and serve on 2 plates with the sauce on top.

KEDGEREE

FISH & SEAFOOD

TIME NEEDED 40 mins

SERVES 4 PEOPLE

Ingredients

6 oz (175 g) long grain rice
6 oz (175 g) cooked fish
4 eggs
3 oz (75 g) butter
4 oz (110 g) mushrooms
½ an onion, finely chopped
1 level teaspoon mild curry powder
3 tablespoons single cream (or top of milk)
salt and pepper

This used to be popular at grand Victorian breakfasts. Now, it makes a quick and easy light lunch or supper dish. It is a good way to make a bit of fish go further - you could use one of the boil-in-the-bag varieties, such as smoked haddock or kippers.

Instructions

Cooking

Cook the rice in boiling salted water for about 12 minutes - so try a few grains to see if done, or follow the instructions on the packet. While the rice is cooking, hard boil the eggs, cool them a little under running water, shell them and chop into small pieces. Melt the butter in a pan, add the curry powder and let it fry for a few seconds; then add the chopped onion and sauté until it softens. Add the sliced mushrooms and let these cook for a few minutes, then take off the heat. Add the flaked fish, chopped hard-boiled egg and the drained rice. Pour the cream over this mixture, stir well to coat, and season to taste. Warm thoroughly in an oven-proof serving dish in a low oven.

VEGETABLE DISHES

HONEYED MARROW

Ingredients

3 tablespoons oil, preferably olive or sunflower

2 cloves garlic, crushed

¼ teaspoon powdered ginger

12 oz (350 g) marrow, peeled, seeded and cubed

2 tablespoons honey

salt and pepper to taste

1 tablespoon sesame seeds

Instructions

Preparation

Heat the oil in a frying pan and add the crushed garlic and ginger.

Cooking

Fry the cubes of marrow in this mixture, turning until it is slightly browned and beginning to go crisp - about 5 minutes. Dribble the honey over the marrow and sprinkle with sesame seeds. Toast under the grill for a couple of minutes.

RATATOUILLE

Ingredients

I courgette
¼ a small onion, roughly chopped
I clove garlic, crushed
I red pepper
I green pepper
I small aubergine
I tablespoon olive oil
I dessertspoon tomato purée
about ¼ pint (275 ml) water
salt and pepper

This southern French vegetable stew can provide a tasty dish on its own, or it makes a good accompaniment to a meat dish.

Instructions

Preparation

Heat the oil in a frying pan, and fry the chopped onion. Add the crushed garlic, and then the other vegetables, sliced thinly.

Cooking

Sauté these, stirring frequently, for about 5 minutes over a gently heat and then add the tomato purée and a little less than ½ pint (275 ml) of water. Mix well together and allow to simmer for 5-10 minutes, stirring frequently, until the vegetables have softened and most of the liquid has evaporated. Season with salt and pepper to taste.

STUFFED AUBERGINE

Ingredients

3 medium aubergines

1 onion, chopped

1 or 2 cloves garlic, crushed

2 teaspoons chopped fresh basil, or 1 teaspoon of dried basil

8 oz (25 g) tin of sardines (optional)

6 oz (175 g) mozzarella cheese

3 large tomatoes, sliced

1½ tablespoons drained capers, chopped

salt and pepper

olive oil for shallow frying

These are good as a starter or a vegetarian main course.

Instructions

Preparation

Trim the stalks from the aubergines and slice in half lengthways. Remove the soft flesh from the aubergine with a grapefruit knife or sharp spoon. Chop the pulp and place in a small bowl. Sprinkle salt on the reserved skins and leave to drain upside down.

Heat the oil in a saucepan and gently fry the onions; stir in the garlic, the aubergine pulp and half the basil. Cook gently for about 10 minutes and then add the chopped sardines (removing any large bones) if you are using them. Season to taste.

STUFFED AUBERGINE

Preparation (continued)

Next dry the aubergine shells with kitchen paper and arrange them on a baking tray. Spoon the aubergine pulp mixture into the shells, arranging alternate slices of cheese and tomato on top of each. Finish with the chopped capers and the remaining chopped basil.

Cooking

Bake at gas mark 5, 375°F (190°C) for 40-45 minutes until cooked thoroughly.

An alternative filling could be made using 4 oz (110 g) of mushrooms and 4 oz (110 g) of roughly chopped pine nuts instead of the sardines. This gives it a very Italian flavour and offers a vegetarian alternative.

BAKED STUFFED TOMATOES

Ingredients

8 large tomatoes

6 tablespoons olive oil

1 large onion, chopped

2 cloves garlic, crushed

6 oz cooked long grain rice

6 tablespoons chopped fresh mint

6 tablespoons tomato purée

2 oz (50 g) feta, Cheshire or Caerphilly cheese

6 tablespoons water

1 tablespoons dried oregano

salt and pepper

Instructions

Preparation

Cut a slice from the top of each tomato and, using a teaspoon or vegetable baller, scoop out the flesh and seeds, taking care not to pierce the walls. Chop the tomato flesh. Heat the oil and fry the onion and garlic over a moderate heat for 3-4 minutes, stirring once or twice. Mix in the chopped tomato, cooked rice, mint and half the tomato purée. Season with salt and pepper to taste. Bring to the boil and cook for 4-5 minutes, stirring occasionally. Taste the mixture and season with a little more pepper if necessary (do not add more salt as the cheese is often quite salty). Stir in the cheese and remove from the heat.

Spoon the filling into the tomato shells. Mix the remaining tomato purée with the water and stir in the oregano and add more seasoning if needed. Pour the sauce around the tomatoes. **(continued)**

(Opposite) Nut loaf with cheese and tomato layer (page 16), herbed chicken with orange (page 25) and Italian flag salad

(Overleaf) Biskotentorte (page 88), ginger meringue with rhubarb sauce (page 84) and carob and orange roulade

BAKED STUFFED TOMATOES

Instructions (continued)

Cooking

Bake in the oven at gas mark 5, 375°F (190°C) for 20-25 minutes until the tops are browned. Serve either hot or cold.

HEDGEHOG POTATOES

VEGETABLE DISH

TIME NEEDED 1¼ hrs

SERVES (SEE RECIPE)

Ingredients

peeled oval potatoes, as many as required
olive oil or butter flavoured with a little crushed garlic

Glynn Christian showed me how to make this recipe; it makes a very pretty dish as the slices open out while roasting so that the potatoes look like small hedgehogs.

Instructions

Preparation

Peel the potatoes and take a slice off the base of each so that they sit flat on the plate or chopping board. Slice the potato downwards several times, cutting almost to the base but without slicing right through.

(Overleaf) Summer pudding (page 79), pears in red wine (page 78) and brown bread ice cream in brandy snap baskets (page 81)

(Opposite) Chocolate courgette cake (page 102), Aztec biscuits (page 104), This morning biscuits (page 107) and florentines (page 104)

Cooking

Put the potatoes in a roasting tin and baste with the oil or flavoured butter. Bake at gas mark 5, 375°F (190°C) for about 1 hour until golden brown.

HOLIDAY PASTA

VEGETABLE DISHES

TIME NEEDED 20 mins

SERVES 2 PEOPLE

Ingredients

4-5 oz (110-115 g) dry pasta per person

the sauce:
2 dessertspoons olive oil
½ large onion, chopped
1 clove garlic, crushed
14 oz (400 g) tin chopped tomatoes
½ glass red wine (optional)
1 tablespoon chopped fresh basil or 1 teaspoon dried
salt and pepper
parmesan cheese to garnish

Instructions

Cooking

Cook the pasta in plenty of salted boiling water until soft but still chewy (the instructions on the packet will give precise cooking times - these differ according to the shape of pasta you are using).

While the pasta is boiling, sauté the onion in the olive oil over a low heat until it goes transparent. Add the garlic and then the tinned chopped tomatoes and the wine if you are using it. Simmer this mixture for about 5 minutes, stirring occasionally until it reduces and thickens into a sauce.

Presentation

Season to taste with salt and pepper, add the basil and stir in. Cook the sauce for half a minute more and serve a generous helping with your pasta. Sprinkle with finely grated parmesan cheese for a really Italian touch.

VEGETABLE RISOTTO

Ingredients

4 oz (110 g) cashew nuts

15 oz (430 g) tin kidney beans

1 red pepper, de-seeded and chopped

1 large or 2 small onions, chopped

4 oz (110 g) mushrooms

2 tablespoons olive oil

salt and pepper

8 oz (225 g) short grain rice, preferably Italian arborio,
    or risotto, rice

small bunch fresh parsley

Instructions

Cooking

Cook the rice in plenty of boiling salted water for 15 minutes or until tender. While it is cooking, heat the oil in a large pan and fry the onion until it starts to brown. Add the red pepper, stir and fry again for another couple of minutes. Rinse the kidney beans under the cold tap and add to the pan with the cashews. Stir well together, chop the parsley and add it to the mixture. Season to taste.

When the rice is cooked, drain well and add it to the pan of vegetables. Stir, check the seasoning and serve immediately.

QUICK CHEESE BEANBURGERS

VEGETABLE DISHES

TIME NEEDED 35 mins

SERVES 3 PEOPLE

Ingredients

15 oz (450 g) can baked beans in tomato sauce
3 oz (75 g) Cheddar cheese
4 oz (110 g) wholewheat bread
½ teaspoon soy sauce
1 small egg, beaten
vegetable oil, preferably groundnut or sunflower

This is a useful recipe if you want to make vegetarian burgers. It really is very easy to make, especially if you have a food processor.

Instructions

Preparation

Drain the beans over a small saucepan. Keep the sauce to serve with the burgers. Mash the beans to a coarse paste, or process in a food processor. Mix the paste with the cheese, breadcrumbs and soy sauce and bind with the egg. Shape the mixture into 6 flat round patties.

Cooking

Brush with the vegetable oil just before cooking under a hot grill (or on a hot barbeque); turn once during the cooking time and brush again with oil. When ready, the burgers should be nicely browned on both sides.

CARROT RING

Ingredients

1 teaspoon oil or butter

1 medium onion, chopped finely

1¼ lb (700 g) carrots, peeled and sliced

½ pint (150 ml) chicken or vegetable stock

1 teaspoon honey

4 oz (110 g) courgettes, sliced

2 tablespoons chopped walnuts

2 eggs

2 oz (50 g) curd or cottage cheese, blended smooth

1 teaspoon dried tarragon

seasoning of salt, pepper or grated nutmeg to taste

Instructions

Cooking

Gently cook the chopped onion in the oil or butter gently for 10 minutes, covered. Add the carrots, stir to mix, then add the stock and the honey. Cover the pan again and cook over a low heat for 20 minutes. Add the courgettes and cook for 5 minutes. Drain off any excess water and either mince the vegetables finely or process in a food blender. Heat the oven to gas mark 5, 375°F (190°C). Grease a 1½ pint (½ litre) ring mould and sprinkle the chopped walnuts in the bottom. Whisk together the eggs, curd cheese, tarragon and seasoning and stir into the vegetable mixture, then spoon into the mould. Tap the mould firmly on a wooden board or table-top to make sure the mixture has shaken down, and cover with kitchen foil. Put the filled and covered mould into a roasting tin and pour hot water around to come halfway up the mould. Bake for about 40 minutes until set firm. Turn out carefully. This dish can be served hot or cold.

GREEK SALAD

VEGETABLE DISHES

TIME NEEDED 10 mins

SERVES 4 PEOPLE

Ingredients

8 oz (225 g) tomatoes

half a cucumber

1 green pepper

1 small bunch spring onions

6 oz (175 g) feta cheese

4 crisp lettuce leaves

3 tablespoons olive oil

1 tablespoon white wine vinegar

several black olives (optional)

salt and pepper

1 dessertspoon chopped fresh marjoram

You can buy feta cheese in most places now, but a white crumbly cheese such as Caerphilly or white Stilton could be used instead.

Instructions

Preparation

Peel the cucumber, de-seed the pepper, and cut both into small cubes. Skin the tomatoes if you wish, and slice or chop them. Clean and slice the spring onions, and roughly chop the lettuce. Combine the oil, wine vinegar, salt and pepper with the marjoram to make a dressing

Presentation

Put the prepared salad ingredients in a bowl, pour the dressing over, and mix well. Crumble the cheese on the top. This can be served as a starter or as a side salad. It would go particularly well with the minted meatballs on page 34.

ITALIAN FLAG SALAD

Ingredients

2 ripe avocado pears
2 beef or 4-6 smaller tomatoes
2 mozzarella cheeses, sold in lumps the size of an apple
fresh basil leaves
a little vinaigrette or French dressing

*This light lunch or starter gets its name from the colours of
the Italian flag which are reflected in the ingredients.*

Instructions

Preparation

Halve, stone and peel the avocado pears. Slice the
tomatoes and the cheese.

Presentation

Arrange slices of avocado, tomato and mozzarella in
rows across a flat serving dish or platter, and drizzle
with a little dressing. Chop the basil leaves and sprinkle
over.

LEEK AND MUSHROOM FILO PARCELS

VEGETABLE DISHES

TIME NEEDED 40 mins

SERVES 4 PEOPLE

Ingredients

3 small leeks, trimmed and thoroughly washed

2 oz (50 g) mushrooms

I oz (25 g) butter

I small onion, finely chopped

12-16 sheets filo pastry

1½ oz (10 g) unsalted butter, melted

Filo pastry, used in Greek and Middle Eastern dishes, can now be bought either frozen or fresh in many supermarkets or specialist grocers.

Instructions

Preparation

Finely chop the leeks. Melt the butter in a saucepan and gently sauté the onion for about 5 minutes until softened. Add the leeks and continue cooking for a further 10 minutes. Season with salt and freshly ground black pepper and allow to cool. Use 3-4 sheets of pastry, one on top of each other, for each parcel. Brush each 'leaf' with melted butter and, keeping the sheets together, cut in half. Place a generous amount of the leek mixture in the middle of each square and gather the corners of the pastry towards the centre. Squeeze gently to make a top knot. Brush with the remaining melted butter. Repeat this process for the remaining parcels.

Cooking

Place on a lightly oiled baking sheet and bake at gas mark 6, 400°F (200°C) for 8 minutes until golden.

SAFFRON SAUCE FOR
LEEK AND MUSHROOM FILO PARCELS

VEGETABLE DISHES

TIME NEEDED 10 mins

SERVES 3 - 4 PEOPLE

Ingredients

8 strands saffron or ½ teaspoon of turmeric
½ pint (275 ml) medium dry white wine
¼ pint (150 ml) double cream or Greek yoghurt

Instructions

Preparation

Put the saffron or turmeric and the wine into a small pan and bring to the boil. Simmer until reduced by half. Season and strain. Stir in 4 fl oz (110 ml) of the cream. Heat very gently.

Presentation

Pour the sauce around the filo parcels and decorate with the remaining cream.

CARROTS WITH THYME

Ingredients

1½ lb (700 g) carrots

a knob of butter

1 tablespoon brown sugar

a squeeze of lemon juice

1 dessertspoon chopped fresh thyme

Instructions

Preparation

Wash and scrape the carrots and cut into sticks. Boil in salted water until just tender. Drain, cover and set aside to keep warm. In a pan (you can use the saucepan the carrots were boiled in) melt the butter, and add the sugar and lemon juice. Stir for a few seconds until mixed, and then add the carrots and the thyme.

Cooking

Cook for about 1 minute over a medium heat, stirring all the time to make sure the carrots are well coated. Serve immediately.

PUDDINGS & DESSERTS

PEARS IN RED WINE

PUDDINGS & DESSERTS

TIME NEEDED 45 mins

SERVES 4 PEOPLE

Ingredients

4 pears
½ pint (275 ml) red wine
½ pint (275 ml) water
2 cloves
1 bay leaf

Instructions

Preparation

Peel the pears and poach them by simmering gently in a pan with the wine, water, cloves and the bay leaf.

Cooking

The length of time the pears take to poach depends on their ripeness, but as a rough guide, 30 minutes is usually plenty. Test to see if they are tender with a skewer. When they are ready, remove the pears from the pan, and boil the liquid to reduce it by half, forming a syrupy sauce.

Presentation

Pour this sauce over the pears, which can be served either warm or slightly chilled.

SUMMER PUDDING

Ingredients

½ lb (225 g) each of 3 types of soft fruits such as raspberries, redcurrants or blackberries (1½ lb, 700 g, in all)

4 oz (110 g) caster sugar

about ½ lb (225 g) white bread slices, crusts removed

This pudding freezes well so it is worth making lots in late summer when fruit is plentiful. You can also make it in winter using frozen fruit.

Instructions

Preparation

Put the prepared fruits in a pan with the sugar and one tablespoon of water and heat gently. Simmer for about 4 minutes until the juices begin to run. Use the slices of bread to line a pudding basin, 1½ pint (¾ litre) size, cutting and filling so that there are no gaps.

Tip the fruit in over the bread to fill almost to the top. Keep back a little juice as there will probably be too much. Cover the fruit with more slices of bread, weigh down with a plate and chill in the fridge for several hours or overnight.

Presentation

When you tip the pudding out, use the reserved juice to moisten any parts of the bread which are not already well soaked and coloured.

RHUBARB ICE CREAM

Ingredients

½ lb rhubarb
sugar to taste - I use 4 oz (110 g)
1 carton Greek yoghurt, 8 oz (225 g) size
2 egg whites

The first sign of spring is when Fred the Weatherman starts telling us how far his rhubarb has sprouted. By the time it's big enough to pick he's run out of ideas for what to do with it and doesn't want anything too fattening. So I came up with this recipe, a no-cream ice cream which doesn't have too many calories so long as you go easy on the sugar.

Instructions

Preparation

Wash and trim the rhubarb, cut into chunks and cook in a pan with the sugar and a minimum of water - one tablespoon - until it falls into a mushy pulp, which should take about 10 minutes. Allow this to cool in the fridge, then whizz it to a smooth pulp in a blender or food processor. Mix the yoghurt thoroughly into this pulp. Whisk the egg whites until stiff, then carefully fold them into the pink rhubarb and yoghurt mixture. Put in the freezer for several hours until firm and move to the fridge about 20 minutes before you want to eat it.

BROWN BREAD ICE-CREAM IN BRANDY SNAP BASKETS

TIME NEEDED 25 mins
+CHILLING

SERVES 4 PEOPLE

Ingredients

4 brandy snaps
3/4 pint (425 ml) double cream
3 oz (75 g) fresh brown breadcrumbs
3 oz (75 g) demerara sugar
2 eggs
1 tablespoon honey
2 tablespoons brandy (optional)

It may sound homely but this is quite my favourite ice cream recipe, and it's smart enough for a party in these easy cheat's baskets.

Instructions

Cooking

Mix the breadcrumbs and sugar together then toast them either in a dry frying pan or in the oven, gas mark 6, 400°F (200°C) turning and mixing frequently with a wooden spoon until the sugar melts into the breadcrumbs and it looks like a dark, crunchy caramel. Separate the eggs and beat the yolks with the honey in a large bowl. Whisk the cream in another bowl until it just holds its shape, and, in a third bowl, whisk the egg whites until stiff. Fold the cream into the egg yolk and honey mixture, mix well, and then carefully fold the stiff egg whites into this. Lastly stir in the cooled sugar and breadcrumb mixture, and the brandy if you are using it. Put into a suitable container and leave in the freezer for several hours or overnight. This ice cream keeps quite well in the freezer for a month or so, but take it out and put in the fridge for 20 minutes before you want to eat it so you can scoop it out easily.

PINEAPPLE CREAM

PUDDINGS & DESSERTS

TIME NEEDED 2 hrs

SERVES 4 PEOPLE

Ingredients

2 oz (50 g) butter

4 oz (110 g) caster sugar

2 eggs

2 oz (50 g) cornflour

7 oz (200 g) tin of pineapple chunks

1 pint (570 ml) milk

Instructions

Preparation

Cream together the butter and half the sugar. Separate the eggs and add the yolks to the creamed mixture. Blend the cornflour to a smooth paste with a little of the milk. Bring the remaining milk to the boil and pour over cornflour mixture. Combine this sauce-like mixture with the butter, sugar and egg yolks to which only the pineapple fruit (not the juice) has been added. Pour into a greased 1 pint (500 ml) dish. Whisk the egg white to stiff peaks and then beat in 1 oz (25 g) of the caster sugar and fold in the remainder.

Cooking

Pile the meringue on top of the pineapple cream and bake at gas mark 1-2 (100°C) for 1-2 hours until meringue is dry and crisp.

CRUNCHY APPLE LAYER

Ingredients

1½ oz (40 g) butter or margarine

4 oz (110 g) fresh brown breadcrumbs

1 teaspoon ground cinnamon

3 oz (75 g) demerara sugar

1 large cooking apple

1 oz (25 g) sultanas

4 oz (110 g) bar plain chocolate

¼ pint (150 ml) whipping cream

5 oz (150 g) carton natural yogurt

Instructions

Preparation

Melt the butter and stir in the breadcrumbs and cinnamon. Cook for about 4 minutes to crisp up and then add half the sugar. Allow to cool and the mixture will become crispier. Peel, core and slice the apple; keep back a couple of slices to decorate and place the rest either in the microwave on high with 2 tablespoons of water and the remainder of the sugar for 2-3 minutes, or, to cook conventionally, cook the apple slices in a saucepan for 4-5 minutes with ¼ pint of water and the sugar. Do not allow to overcook or you will lose the shape of the slices.

Whip the cream and yoghurt together until they fold a mixture with soft peaks then fold in the melted chocolate. Place a spoonful of this chocolate cream in the base of each glass. Cover with a layer of breadcrumbs then one of apple; continue in layers ending with the crisp breadcrumbs. Chill the desserts for at least 4 hours, or overnight.

GINGER MERINGUES
WITH RHUBARB SAUCE

Ingredients

4 egg whites

8 oz (225 g) caster sugar

4 teasspoons (30 ml) finely chopped preserved stem ginger

2 teaspoons (10 ml) preserved stem ginger syrup

10 fl oz (284 ml) rhubarb

2 oz (50 g) granulated sugar

1 level teaspoon (5 ml) arrowroot

icing sugar to decorate

Instructions

Preparation

Line two baking sheets with non-stick baking parchment. Whisk the egg whites until stiff but not dry. Add 2 level tablespoons (30 ml) of the caster sugar and whisk again until very stiff and shiny. Fold in the remmaining caster sugar. Spoon or pipe the meringue mixture into 48 walnut-sized rounds, well spaced on the baking sheets.

Cooking

Bake at gas mark ½ 250°F (130°C) for about 2 hours. Cool slightly and the purée. Blend the arrowroot with 1 tablespoon (15 ml) water and stir into the rhubarb purée. Bring to the boil, stirring for 1-2 minutes until thickened. Cool.

Presentation

To serve the meringues, sandwich the rounds together with a little of the ginger cream. Refrigerate for about 30 minutes to soften slightly. Dust with icing sugar and serve with the rhubarb sauce.

CINNAMON SPICE BANANAS

Ingredients

1 firm banana
1 teaspoon butter
1 teaspoon lemon juice
1 teaspoon brown sugar or clear honey
a pinch of cinnamon
a dash of rum or brandy

Instructions

Preparation

Peel the banana and cut lengthways into thick slices. Place on a double thickness of aluminium foil and add the brown sugar or honey and dust with the cinnamon.

Cooking

Dot the banana with the butter, wrap the edges of the foil securely and bake in a moderate oven, gas mark 5, 375°F (190°C) for about 10 minutes until soft.

QUICK AND EASY CHEESECAKE

Ingredients

Base:
8 oz (225 g) digestive biscuits, crushed
4 oz (110 g) butter or margarine
2 oz (50 g) toasted hazlenuts (optional)

Filling:
8 oz (225 g) cottage cheese
2 oz (50 g) sugar
1 oz (25 g) self-raising flour
2 eggs
juice of 1 lemon or lime

Decoration:
grapes or slices of lemon

Instructions

Preparation

Lightly grease a loose-bottomed cake tin or flan dish. Melt the butter or margarine and mix with the crushed digestive biscuits and chopped toasted hazlenuts if you are using them. Press into the prepared dish.
Blend together all the ingredients for the filling. Pour the filling into the biscuit base.

Cooking

Bake at gas mark 4-5, 350°F (180°C) for approximately 30 minutes, or until set. When cooked, turn off the oven but leave the cheesecake inside to cool slowly - this way you avoid too many cracks developing.

Presentation

Decorate as desired with grapes or lemon slices, and, if you want, some whipped cream.

PECAN PIE

TIME NEEDED 1 hr

SERVES 6 PEOPLE

Ingredients

8 oz (225 g) shortcrust pastry

2 eggs

8 fl oz (225 ml) golden syrup

4 oz (110 g) dark brown sugar

½ teaspoon vanilla essence

4 oz (110 g) pecan nuts (or walnuts)

This is an American classic - if you have difficulty finding pecans, walnuts are equally tasty.

Instructions

Preparation

Grease an 8 or 9 inch (20 or 23 cm) flan dish and line with the rolled out pastry. Bake 'blind' for 20 minutes at gas mark 6, 400°F (200°C).

Beat the eggs together in a bowl, add the golden syrup, sugar and vanilla essence and beat again. Mix in the nuts and pour the filling into the pastry case.

Cooking

Lower the oven temperature to gas mark 4, 350°F (180°C) and bake the pie for 45 minutes if you are using a shallow 9 inch (23 cm) dish, or for 1 hour if using a deeper 8 inch (20 cm) dish. When the pie is ready the filling is just set and the pastry nicely golden.

Presentation

Serve either hot or cold - it is delicious with vanilla ice cream, or you even could try it with Greek yoghurt.

BISKOTENTORTE
A COFFEE, ORANGE & WALNUT SENSATION

PUDDINGS & DESSERTS

TIME NEEDED 45 mins

SERVES 6 PEOPLE

Ingredients

2 packets sponge fingers

7 oz (200 g) butter

6 oz (150 g) sugar

1 egg

½ oz (110 g) walnuts, chopped

1 oz (25 g) flour

½ pint (125 ml) milk

1 oz (25 g) instant coffee

1 glass sherry

1 glass pure orange juice

whipped cream to decorate (optional)

Instructions

Preparation

Lightly grease a 7 inch deep cake tin (preferably with a removable base). Cream 6 oz (150 g) of the butter, with the sugar, egg and chopped nuts.

Cooking

Make a roux by melting the remaining 1 oz (25 g) of butter and carefully blending the flour into this. Cook for a few minutes then remove from the heat and gradually add the milk. Mix a small amount of water with the instant coffee to form a paste; blend this into the mixture and allow to cool. Carefully add the roux mixture a spoonful at a time to the creamed butter and sugar. Mix together the orange juice and sherry, and quickly dip the sponge fingers into this and place them around the sides of the prepared cake tin, with the rounded sides towards the outside.

BISKOTENTORTE

Instructions

Cooking

Fill the centre of the cake with a layer of coffee mixture and a layer of soaked sponge fingers. Allow to set.

Presentation

Turn out and decorate with whipped cream and nuts, if desired.

ATHOLL BROSE

PUDDINGS

TIME NEEDED 25 mins

SERVES 4 PEOPLE

Ingredients

½ pint (275 g) double cream
2 heaped tablespoons medium oatmeal
I generous tablespoon honey
2 tablespoons whisky

There are many variations of this old Scottish recipe, and this is mine. I don't know if it is authentic, but it is very rich and everyone seems to like it.

Instructions

Preparation

Toast the oatmeal until it goes a golden brown - you can do this in a deep frying pan, turning it with a wooden spoon. Set aside to cool. Whisk the cream, honey and whisky together until thick. Fold in two thirds of the oatmeal and pile into the serving glasses or bowls. Sprinkle the remaining oatmeal on top.

QUEEN OF PUDDINGS

TIME NEEDED 2 hrs

SERVES 4 PEOPLE

Ingredients

5 oz (150 g) breadcrumbs

1 oz (25 g) sugar

1 teaspoon lemon juice

1 pint (570 ml) milk

2 oz (50 g) butter

4 eggs

4 tablespoons red jam

4 oz (110 g) caster sugar

Instructions

Preparation

Heat the milk and butter in a pan until warm. Put the breadcrumbs, lemon juice and 1 oz (25 g) of the sugar in a bowl. Add the warmed milk and butter and leave to stand for few minutes. Meanwhile, separate the eggs and beat the yolks into the crumb mixture.

Cooking

Pour this into a fairly deep, greased pie dish and bake at gas mark 4, 350°F (180°C) until just firm - this should take about an hour and a half. Gently spread the jam over the surface of the pudding - it will spread more easily if you warm it slightly first.

Presentation

Make a meringue topping by whisking the egg whites until they form stiff peaks; fold in the remaining caster sugar and spread on top of the jam. Put back in the oven for approximately 10 minutes to brown the meringue.

SUSSEX POND PUDDING

PUDDINGS & DESSERTS

TIME NEEDED 2 - 2½ hrs

SERVES 4 - 6 PEOPLE

Ingredients

6 oz (175 g) self-raising flour

3 oz (75 g) shredded suet

a good pinch of salt

4 fl oz (110 ml) water

3 oz (75 g) butter

3 oz (75 g) demerara sugar

1 lemon, thick-skinned if possible

It's magic - you just wouldn't believe you could eat a whole lemon, rind and all, but just try it and see!

Instructions

Preparation

Lightly oil a 2 pint (1 litre) pudding basin - I use my middle sized Pyrex bowl. Mix the flour, salt and suet with the water to form a soft dough. Reserve a quarter of the dough for a lid and roll out the rest on a well-floured surface, and use to line the pudding bowl.
Put a few flakes of butter and a sprinkling of the sugar in the bottom of the pie. Wash the lemon, prick it all over with a fork and place it in the bowl. Add the rest of the sugar and the butter, cut into small pieces, around the lemon.

Cooking

Roll out the reserved pastry to make a lid and fit it over the top, tucking in any spare edges and pressing down neatly. If you have a microwave, cook on high for 10 minutes, then let it rest for 10 minutes before turning out. Alternatively, steam the pudding for about 2½ hours.

BAKED ALASKA

PUDDINGS & DESSERTS

TIME NEEDED 40 mins

SERVES 4 - 5 PEOPLE

Ingredients

a sponge base, either round or rectangular, a little larger than the block of ice cream
a large block of ice cream - choose your favourite flavour
a little orange juice or sherry
½ lb (225 g) fresh or tinned fruit
3 egg whites
4 oz (110 g) caster sugar

It seems like magic to find cold ice cream inside a warm cooked meringue - this is definitely one to make at the last minute.

Instructions

Preparation

Keep the ice cream in the freezer while you assemble the other ingredients and make the meringue. To do this, whisk the egg whites until stiff and fold in the sugar. Heat your oven to its hottest temperature. Put the sponge base on an oven-proof dish or plate, and moisten with a little orange juice or sherry. Peel and chop the fresh fruit, or drain the tinned; put about half the fruit over the sponge base and then place the ice cream on top. Pile the rest of the fruit on top of and around the ice cream, then cover this mound with a thick coating of meringue mixture, making sure that you also cover the sides of the sponge base.

Cooking

Put into your very hot oven for 3 minutes so that the meringue is browned but the ice cream remains cold. Serve immediately.

CHOCOLATE FLAKE POCKETS

Ingredients

3 eggs
3 oz (75 g) caster sugar
3 oz (75 g) plain flour
½ teaspoon baking powder

Decoration:
8 fl oz (220 ml) double cream
5 fl oz (150 ml) plain yoghurt
fresh strawberries
3 chocolate flakes

Instructions

Preparation

Pre-heat the oven to gas mark 7, 425°F (220°C). Cover a baking sheet with non-stick parchment. Whisk the eggs and sugar together until pale and creamy. Sift and fold in the flour. Spread the mixture into 6 inch circles.

Cooking

Cook for 4-5 minutes until golden brown. Cover with a damp towel to keep the sponge pliable. When cooled slightly, fill with whipped cream and yoghurt and fold over like an omelette.

Presentation

Decorate with pieces of chocolate flake and some strawberries.

CRÊPES SUSAN

PUDDINGS & DESSERTS

TIME NEEDED 30 mins

SERVES 8 PEOPLE

Ingredients

Crêpes:
4 oz (110 g) plain wholemeal flour
¼ teaspoon salt
1 egg
½ pint (275 ml) milk
a little oil for frying

Filling:
1 small tin apricots
1 carton Greek yoghurt

Sauce:
1 oz (25 g) flaked almonds
1 oz (25 g) butter
the juice from the tinned apricots
2 level dessertspoons brown sugar
apricot brandy (optional)

The amounts in this recipe serve 8 people, as I discovered one evening when all the family were at home, plus a few friends. You could halve the amounts for the filling and sauce, but make all the crêpes because you can't easily halve an egg.

CRÊPES SUSAN

Instructions

Preparation

Combine the flour, salt, milk and the egg by beating to a smooth batter. Heat 2 teaspoons of oil in a small frying pan until very hot, and cook a little batter at a time to make 8 pancakes - add just one teaspoon of oil for each pancake. I find it takes about 30 seconds on the first side, and just 15 on the second. Keep the crêpes warm while preparing the filling and sauce.

Drain the apricots but keep the juice. Chop them fairly small, and mix into the yoghurt.

Divide the filling among the crêpes; spread it over half the circle and roll up. In a large frying pan, melt the butter and gently toast the flaked almonds in it, turning until they start to brown. Add the sugar and some of the juice from the tinned apricots.

Cooking

Put the rolled crêpes into the pan to warm through and spoon the juice over them, keeping them over on a gentle heat for about 3 minutes.

Presentation

If you are using the apricot brandy, warm about 4 tablespoons in a small pan and pour this over the crêpes as you bring it to the table, apply a match to light it to flare, and mind your eyebrows!

CAROB AND ORANGE ROULADE

Ingredients

4 eggs (size 2)

4 oz (110 g) golden granulated sugar

¼ pint (150 ml) milk

2-3 tablespoons carob powder

7½ fl oz (200 ml) double cream or Greek yoghurt

½ teaspoon vanilla essence

juice of 1 orange

grated rind of 3 oranges

Decoration:

2-3 slices of oranges

icing sugar

extra whipped cream

carob chocolate leaves

Carob is a healthy and unusual alternative to chocolate, particularly useful for those who may suffer from migraine.

Instructions

Preparation

Preheat the oven to gas mark 4, 350°F (180°C). Grease and line a 8 x 12 inch (20.5 x 30.5 cm) swiss roll tin. Dissolve the carob powder in some warm milk; when it is smooth, allow to cool. Whisk the carob mixture and the sugar into the egg yolks and add two thirds of the grated orange rind.

Beat the egg whites until they are stiff and fold them into the carob mixture.

CAROB AND ORANGE ROULADE

Instructions

Cooking

Spread this mixture evenly over the swiss roll tray and bake for 15-20 minutes until it is well risen and firm. Turn the roulade out onto a sheet of non-stick parchment. Cover with a warm damp cloth to stop it drying out. Leave to cool.

Presentation

Mix the remaining orange rind, the orange juice and the vanilla essence. Spread this mixture over the roulade and then roll carefully. Don't try to roll it too tightly and don't worry if it cracks slightly. Decorate with piped cream or a line of yoghurt and add some orange peel and carob chocolate leaves.

PANCAKES
STRAWBERRY & CHOCOLATE

PUDDINGS & DESSERTS

TIME NEEDED 1hr

SERVES 6 PEOPLE

Ingredients

Pancake batter:
4 oz (110 g) plain flour
1 egg
¼ pint (150 ml) milk

Filling:
½ lb (225 g) fresh strawberries
2 oz (50 g) caster sugar
2 oz (50 g) butter
¼ pint (150 ml) fresh orange juice
1 teaspoon cornflour

Chocolate sauce:
¼ lb (225 g) milk cooking chocolate, grated or finely chopped
1 pint (570 ml) double cream
1 tot chocolate liqueur

To decorate:
4 whole strawberries
4 fresh mint leaves
lemon juice
icing sugar for dusting

Instructions

Preparation

To make the pancakes, beat together the egg and the milk. Put the flour in a bowl, make a well in the centre and add a quarter of the egg and milk mixture. Blend together, beating carefully.

PANCAKES
STRAWBERRY & CHOCOLATE

Instructions

Preparation (continued)

As the flour absorbs the liquid, add the remainder of the milk and egg and continue beating until you get a smooth batter. Add the water and beat in. Set to one side for 30 minutes. Then make the pancakes and keep them warm.

Cooking

To make the filling, melt the butter in a frying pan, add the sugar and mix in well. Stirring constantly, keep on the heat until the sugar starts to caramelise. Slowly add half the orange juice and mix it in well. Set aside 4 whole strawberries for decorating at the end, and halve the rest. Add them to the caramel mixture and cook them lightly, gradually adding the remainder of the orange juice. Blend the cornflour with a little water and add it to the mixture. Once the mixture has thickened, remove it from the heat.

Next, make the chocolate sauce. Gently bring the cream to the boil, remove from the heat and add the chocolate, stirring until melted and smooth. Add the liqueur and set to one side.

Presentation

To serve, put a generous amount of strawberry filling on one half of each pancake and fold over. Cover the bottom of a warmed plate with some chocolate sauce and put the pancake on top. Garnish with a fan of strawberry, fresh mint leaf and a little lemon juice. Dust with icing sugar as a finishing touch.

PINEAPPLE TRUFFLE LOAF

PUDDINGS & DESSERTS

TIME NEEDED 30 mins
+CHILLING

SERVES 12 PEOPLE

Ingredients

12 oz (350 g) fresh trimmed pineapple (½ a large pineapple)

4 tablespoons dark rum

1 teaspoon vanilla essence

8 oz (225 g) plain chocolate

6 oz (175 g) solid cream of coconut

4 oz (110 g) unsalted butter

7 oz (200 g) gingernut biscuits

This is a slicing dessert that can be presented as simply or as dramatically as you choose. Don't use tinned pineapple or you will miss the sweet-sharpness of the fresh pineapple that is now available all year round.

Instructions

Preparation

Chop the pineapple into small chunks and marinate in the rum and vanilla essence for a couple of hours. Melt together the chocolate, cream of coconut and butter over a gentle heat. Crush the gingernut biscuits finely and stir into the warm mixture, making sure the pieces are evenly distributed. Mix in the rum and vanilla marinade, and then add the pineapple, reserving a little for decorating at the end if you wish.

Pile the mixture into a 2 lb (900 g) loaf tin that has been greased and strip-lined with a double layer of greaseproof paper. Press down lightly to ensure that the mixture is even. Cover and chill overnight or longer. Turn out and slice thinly. Serve very cold, perhaps decorated with a little marinaded pineapple and whipped cream.

CAKES & BISCUITS

CHOCOLATE COURGETTE CAKE

CAKES & BISCUITS

TIME NEEDED 1½ hrs

SERVES 6 - 8 PEOPLE

Ingredients

6 oz (175 g) plain chocolate

7 oz (200 g) self-raising flour

½ teaspoon salt

4 oz (110 g) caster sugar

2 eggs

6 fl oz (150 ml) vegetable oil

8 oz (225 g) courgettes, peeled weight

2 oz (50 g) chopped walnuts

This makes a lovely moist cake and I've found it a useful way of using up a glut of courgettes. It tastes even better the next day but I can't tell you how long it lasts because it's so popular it all gets eaten up very quickly!

Instructions

Preparation

Set the oven to gas mark 4-5, 360°F (180°C). Grease and flour an 8 inch round tin. Melt the chocolate, and grate the peeled courgettes. Whisk the eggs and oil together. Put all the dry ingredients (flour, salt, sugar) into a large bowl, mix in the egg and oil and beat well. Add the chocolate, grated courgettes and chopped nuts and stir well together.

Cooking

Pour into the prepared tin, and bake for about an hour or more until well risen, firm and springly to the touch. Leave to cool in the tin for 10 minutes before turning out onto a wire rack to cool. The cake can be sandwiched or covered with chocolate butter icing.

LEBANESE BANANA CAKE

CAKES & BISCUITS

TIME NEEDED 2 hrs

SERVES 6 - 8 PEOPLE

Ingredients

4 oz (110 g) butter

4 oz (110 g) caster sugar

2 eggs

a pinch of salt

5 tablespoons plain yoghurt

2 tablespoons rosewater (available at most chemists)

2 bananas, peeled and thinly sliced

8 oz (225 g) self-raising flour

½ teaspoon bicarbonate of soda

1 oz (25 g) chopped almonds

icing sugar to decorate

Instructions

Preparation

Cream the butter and sugar together until light and fluffy. Whisk the eggs with the salt, then gradually beat them into the creamed mixture. Beat in the yoghurt and the rosewater, then very gently stir in the sliced banana. Add the sifted flour, bicarbonate of soda and the almonds, and again stir very gently.

Cooking

Grease and flour a 7 inch round cake tin, spoon in the mixture, and leave it to rest for 30 minutes to draw out the flavours. Heat the oven to gas mark 4, 350°F (180°C) and bake the cake for about 1 hour. You should be able to tell when it is cooked when a thin knife or skewer comes out clean from the centre. When cool, sift a little icing sugar over the surface.

FLORENTINES

CAKES & BISCUITS

TIME NEEDED 30 mins

MAKES 30 - 40

Ingredients

4 oz (110 g) butter

3 oz (75 g) caster sugar

1 tablespoon double cream

4 oz (110 g) flaked almonds

2 oz (50 g) chopped candied peel or raisins

2 oz (50 g) glacé cherries, quartered

6 oz plain or white chocolate, or 3 oz (75 g) of each

This recipe should make 30-40, depending on how big you make each biscuit.

Instructions

Preparation

Melt the butter in a pan, add the sugar and heat gently, stirring until it dissolves. Add the cream, bring the mixture to the boil, and let it bubble gently for 1 minute, stirring continuously.
Add the cherries, nuts and the peel or raisins, and stir well together. Using 2 teaspoons, put small amounts on to non-stick parchment on baking trays, leaving plenty of room to spread.

Cooking

Bake each trayful for 5-8 minutes at gas mark 4, 350°F (180°C) until just golden. Remove the biscuits from the oven and push each little shape into a neat round using a spatula. When cool, coat the bottom of each one with the chocolate, melted in a bowl in a pan of hot water; use either white or dark or some of each. Leave to set and serve at teatime or as a party treat.

CARAMEL GINGERBREAD

Ingredients

5 oz (150 g) butter or margarine

6 oz (175 g) black treacle

4 oz (110 g) brown sugar

2 eggs

1 tablespoon water

7 oz (200 g) self-raising flour

2 teaspoons powdered ginger

We always have a sticky dark cake for bonfire night. This one is a good choice because it's not too messy for gloved hands.

Instructions

Preparation

Set the oven to gas mark 4, 350°F (180°C). To make the gingerbread put the water, butter, sugar and treacle into a pan and heat very gently until the butter has melted. Whisk the eggs together in a large bowl then add the flour and ginger. Add the melted ingredients and the eggs and mix well together.

Cooking

Pour the mixture into a greased and lined 8 inch square tin and bake for an hour. The cake has a nice shiny top when done so I split it and pour the caramel filling in the middle. To make this, melt the brown sugar and butter in a pan very gently without boiling until the sugar has all melted, then add the milk and keep stirring for another minute over gentle heat. Pour into a bowl and add the vanilla, then gradually beat in the sifted icing sugar.

CHOCOLATE AZTEC BISCUITS

Ingredients

3 oz (75 g) cornflakes
6 oz (175 g) butter
7 oz (200 g) plain chocolate
6 oz (175 g) plain flour
1 tablespoon cocoa powder
24 walnut halves

These biscuits look very expensive and are good for special occasions, they are actually very easy to make.

Instructions

Preparation

Warm the cornflakes to ensure they are crisp and dry and then crush them fairly freely. Beat the butter and sugar together until light and fluffy.

Melt half the chocolate in a bowl over hot water or in the microwave, and then beat in the butter and sugar. Stir in the sifted flour, cocoa and, finally, add the crushed cornflakes.

Cooking

Put a teaspoon of the mixture onto greased baking trays - about 12 per tray. Bake in a moderate oven, gas mark 4, 350°F (180°C), for about 15 minutes. Allow the biscuits to cool for about 10 minutes before removing them from the tray.

Presentation

Melt the remaining chocolate, drizzle a little onto each biscuit and top with a walnut half.

THIS MORNING BISCUITS

CAKES & BISCUITS

TIME NEEDED 35 mins

SERVES 8 - 10 PEOPLE

Ingredients

4 oz (110 g) butter or margarine
1 ½ oz (40 g) icing sugar
a few drops of vanilla essence
2 oz (50 g) self-raising flour
2 oz (50 g) cornflour

Instructions

Preparation

Cream together the butter and icing sugar with the vanilla essence until you have a soft mixture. Mix in the flour and the cornflour.

With floured hands, roll the mixture into small balls and put them onto a well-greased baking tray – make sure they are spaced out as they spread as they cook. Bake for 1¼ hours in a moderate oven, gas mark 2-3, 315°F (160°C) until the biscuits are golden – about 15-20 minutes. When cool, they should lift off the tray without difficulty.

Presentation

Decoration ideas:
When cool, dip half of each biscuit into melted chocolate, or sprinkle a few toasted flaked almonds on top of each flattened ball before baking. Alternatively, you could press half a glacé cherry on to the top of each biscuit before putting them in the oven.

CHOCOLATE CHESTNUT GATEAU

CAKES & BISCUITS

TIME NEEDED 1 hr

SERVES 8 PEOPLE

Ingredients

4 oz (110 g) plain chocolate

6 oz (175 g) soft margarine

6 oz (175 g) caster sugar

15 oz (400 g) tin chestnut purée

3 eggs

4 tablespoons milk

6 oz (175 g) self-raising flour

3 tablespoons redcurrant jelly

¼ pint (75 ml) single cream

¼ pint (75 ml) double cream

3 oz (75 g) green grapes, halved

2 oz (50 g) redcurrants

I have used grapes and redcurrants for this unusual cake, but you can vary the fruit, choosing your own favourite combinations.

Instructions

Preparation

Cream together the margarine, sugar and two generous spoonfuls of chestnut purée until smooth. Add the eggs to half the milk, and fold in the sifted flour. Turn into a 7½ inch dish which has been greased and base-lined.

CHOCOLATE CHESTNUT GATEAU

Instructions

Cooking

If you are using a conventional oven, bake at gas mark 4, 350°F (180°C) for 30-40 minutes. If you prefer to cook this in a microwave, first make sure that your dish is suitable. Cook on high for 8 minutes, rotating the dish every 2 minutes. Leave to stand for 5 minutes before turning out onto a wire rack. Slice the cake layers back together with about a third of the chocolate cream in between each. Cover the top and sides with the remainder.

Presentation

Decorate with pieces of fresh fruit, such as the grapes and redcurrants.

CHOCOLATE PLANTATION LOAF

CAKES & BISCUITS

TIME NEEDED 1½ hrs

SERVES 6 - 8 PEOPLE

Ingredients

2 small ripe bananas

4 oz (110 g) soft margarine

4 oz (110 g) dark soft brown sugar

1 teaspoon vanilla or rum essence

2 eggs

2 tablespoons milk

8 oz (225 g) plain chocolate

6 oz (175 g) self-raising flour

½ level teaspoon bicarbonate of soda

To complete:

2 small ripe bananas

1 teaspoon lemon juice

2oz (50 g) sifted icing sugar

2 oz (50 g) ground almonds

1 teaspoon flavourless salad oil, such as grapeseed

1 oz (25 g) caster sugar

Instructions

Preparation

Mash the bananas and then beat them with the margarine, sugar and vanilla or rum essence until the mixture is light and creamy. Gradually add the eggs and the milk. Chop the chocolate into small chips and fold it into the mixture with the sieved dry ingredients. Turn into a 2 lb glass or microwave dish, greased and strip-lined.

CHOCOLATE PLANTATION LOAF

Instructions

Cooking

If you have a microwave, cook on high for 7 minutes, rotating the dish every couple of minutes; leave to stand for 5 minutes before turning out to cool on a wire rack covered with cling film. Alternatively, cook in a conventional oven at gas mark 7, 425°F (220°C) for 45 minutes.

Make the filling by mashing one banana with lemon juice, then fold in the icing sugar and ground almonds. Slice the cooled cake in half through the centre and spread the filling on the bottom half before sandwiching together again. Place the remaining chocolate in a bowl with the oil, sugar and 2 tablespoons of water, then either microwave on defrost for 3 minutes or melt in a pan over a gentle heat, stirring until smooth. Leave until it is thick enough to coat the back of a spoon then pour the sauce over the cake, allowing the icing to drip down the sides.

Presentation

Decorate with slices of banana dipped in lemon juice, and serve with yoghurt or cream, as you like.

INDEX